PREGNANT
GIRL

PREGNANT GIRL

A STORY OF
TEEN MOTHERHOOD, COLLEGE,
AND CREATING A BETTER FUTURE
FOR YOUNG FAMILIES

Nicole Lynn Lewis

BEACON PRESS
BOSTON

BEACON PRESS
Boston, Massachusetts
www.beacon.org

Beacon Press books
are published under the auspices of
the Unitarian Universalist Association of Congregations.

This book is printed on acid-free paper that meets the uncoated paper
ANSI/NISO specifications for permanence as revised in 1992.

Text design and composition by Kim Arney

This is a work of nonfiction. All of the incidents reported took place as
recorded here, to the best of my recollection and records. I have changed
the name of only four individuals in the book to protect their privacy.

Library of Congress Cataloging-in-Publication Data
Name: Lewis, Nicole Lynn, author.
Title: Pregnant girl : a story of teen motherhood, college, and creating
a better future for young families / Nicole Lynn Lewis.
Description: Boston, Massachusetts : Beacon Press, 2021. |
Includes bibliographical references.
Identifiers: LCCN 2020057222 (print) | LCCN 2020057223 (ebook) |
ISBN 9780807055618 (paperback) | ISBN 9780807056066 (ebook)
Subjects: LCSH: Teenage mothers—United States. | Young families—United
States. | Teenage parents—United States. | Teenage pregnancy—United States.
Classification: LCC HQ759.4 .L49 2021 (print) | LCC HQ759.4 (ebook) |
DDC 306.874/3—dc23
LC record available at https://lccn.loc.gov/2020057222
LC ebook record available at https://lccn.loc.gov/2020057223

To Pooh Bear, Papaya, Pumpkin, Bean,
and the tiny bit of magic that is growing inside of me.
May your adventures be the things that
dreams are made of.

CONTENTS

PART ONE ▪ EXPECTING

CHAPTER 1 The First Bead 3

CHAPTER 2 Women's Work 22

CHAPTER 3 Love Song 29

CHAPTER 4 Two Pink Lines 42

CHAPTER 5 Into the Dark 60

CHAPTER 6 Red 73

CHAPTER 7 Place 84

CHAPTER 8 A Soul Melting on Hot Pavement. 100

PART TWO ▪ THE URGE TO PUSH

CHAPTER 9 The Strength in Between 111

CHAPTER 10 All Good Things 122

CHAPTER 11 Freedom Dance 134

CHAPTER 12 Taking Shape 147

CHAPTER 13 Honors 158

PART THREE ▪ CROWNING

CHAPTER 14 Inheritance 169

CHAPTER 15 Breech 176

CHAPTER 16 CEO 184

CHAPTER 17 Peace 194

Acknowledgments 197

Notes 200

PART ONE

EXPECTING

THE FIRST BEAD

CRACK SMELLS LIKE a soul melting on hot pavement. Crackling. Popping. Hissing. The burnt stench sticks with you. No scrubbing can wash it away. It is an instant and irreversible invitation into another world—a dark world—that will forever change the way you look at life. The first and last time I saw a crack pipe I was nineteen years old and five months pregnant. I was sitting in the passenger seat of a black Ford Explorer, watching trees and stores blur by. Stacey was driving—driving and smoking crack.

By then, I'd mastered the survival mechanism of avoiding the things that scared me the most. Facing those things, I determined, made them more real and gave them a credibility that required action. To avoid them, to look at objects that were connected to them rather than the very thing, veiled the ugly truth of a person or situation.

So, I didn't look at Stacey's face. Besides, I knew what I would find. I had seen it before. It would be a sunken, hollow, ghostlike mask. Her brown eyes would be vacant, her pupils dilated. Instead, I glanced at the one hand she used to move the steering wheel, red chipped nail polish and pipe burns on every other finger. I found the other hand. With unwavering determination, she was using it to steady the crack pipe to her lips. In seconds, she would be a euphoric burst of energy. This would be the not-so-bad side of Stacey's high. Energetic and exuberant for five to ten minutes as the drug traveled from her lungs straight into her bloodstream. Later that night, I might see the bad side—her insomnia, her screaming about the bugs crawling under her skin, or her incessant phone calls to find the next tiny bag of small, pale-rose-colored rocks.

She'd asked me if I wanted to ride somewhere with her, and even though I didn't know where we were going or if I would be safe, I said yes. I was convinced any place would be better than her dark apartment, where I spent most of my days alone. Now we were riding around Norfolk, Virginia, while she got high and the cops could pull us over any minute.

At a red light, she closed her eyes and rested her head back against the seat. Her shiny brown hair hadn't been washed or combed in days, her lips dry and peeling. She was enjoying the sensation traveling through her body.

The burnt stench filled the car and seeped into my clothes and hair. I held my breath, but it crept in through my nose anyway. My belly turned, the nausea making me shift awkwardly in my seat. I rolled down the window to take in something normal—the baby-blue sky, the green grass sprouting through the cracks in the sidewalk.

A tall Black man on the median selling bottles of water for a dollar caught my eye. His T-shirt read "Jesus Saves," and there were small patches of silver hair on his unshaven face. The two circles of sweat underneath each arm showed he'd been standing in the hot sun for a while. He raised a bottle toward me and then slowly lowered his arm when he saw my face. Then the honking cars behind us woke Stacey up, and she sped off.

This was it. There had been horrible moments before this when I hardly recognized myself, and there would be more to come. But right then, in that car with Stacey, this was the most crushing departure from who I was and who I wanted to be. Worst of all, my unborn baby was along for the ride. This was unquestionably *rock bottom*.

But even in that moment, I looked at Stacey and thought I was at least better off than she was. I'd never even smoked weed or cigarettes or drank alcohol. I was still young, and even though I was going to be a mother, there was still a slim chance I might go to college and do something with

my life. I was an honor roll student. I was smart. There was just this pregnancy. That was it. That's the one thing I had to overcome.

Now I understand this was a naive, simplistic view of the world and
the places that Stacey and I occupied in it. Even as an addict on the verge
of being homeless, Stacey's prospects were far better than mine. As a
White woman, her chances of accessing the supports needed to survive
her addiction, go to college, and work in a well-paid, fulfilling career
were pretty high. If she didn't want to go to college, she could always
work for her father and maybe one day inherit his successful car dealership. If she decided to have children, she would be three to four times less
likely than me to die in childbirth.[1] No one would ever know by looking
at her or reviewing her resume that she had once been addicted to crack.
In fact, she would generally be able to move through the world with people assuming the best about her.

Things would be different for me, as a pregnant Black teenager,
even with a White mother. Regardless of how smart I was or how hard I
worked, supports that could really make a difference for me and my child
would be guarded by unnecessary barriers, and a college degree would be
an evasive ever-moving target, meant for someone else. The idea of not
going to college and still being able to provide for my family wasn't a viable one, yet even a degree would not erase the glaring wealth gap handed
down from generation to generation in my family. In the hospital, when
it was time for me to give birth, nurses would assume I had a history of
drugs because of my age and the color of my skin. When my daughter
arrived, there would be no hiding the fact that I was a teen mother. Her
existence would be an invitation for people's judgment, scrutiny, and disdain, even after I earned two degrees, and no matter how bright and full
of light my child would be. Unlike Stacey, I would move through the
world with people assuming the worst about me, constantly wanting me
to prove my worthiness. Was I worthy of resources? Was I worthy of
opportunities? Was I worthy of an education? I would see this play out
for me and the countless young mothers and fathers I would work with
in the years to come.

I would learn that we have much to overcome.

·　·　·　·　·

When I was little, maybe eight years old, I would lie down in the back seat of my parents' red 1979 Chevy Monza and look up through the window. Underneath me and draped across the seats were bright colored, striped towels that were first used to protect our legs from the hot, black leather that would sear our skin in the summer but were now there to preserve the cracking, old leather beneath. This was the plan until they could afford a new car. I could hear the two of them immersed in some philosophical conversation about my mother's artwork or a new jazz musician as they drove along. Fleshing out metaphors for the human struggle, debating the deeper meaning in a painting or a song.

Their words usually danced through the air to the crescendo and downswing of a saxophone while my mind raced. I was a dreamer—always a dreamer. I'd picture myself as a grown-up, wearing a business suit and clutching a briefcase. I was thin with long flowing hair. Sophisticated. Or maybe I was on a stage in front of thousands of adoring fans, singing so passionately into a microphone you could see the raised veins on the side of my neck, just like Whitney Houston's. Other times, I was in another country—Africa, maybe—reading to little children in a village. My dreams were big.

And other times, my dreams were small, quiet stories that I wrapped just as tightly around my heart. I imagined one day I would marry a tall, dark, and handsome man, and we'd have a house full of babies. I rehearsed this scenario with my Barbie dolls, who lived in a modest shoebox in my side of the closet, with their My Little Pony children. I happily cooked all the meals, kept the shoebox clean, lovingly brushed their pink and purple hair, and then kissed each of them while tucking them into bed at night. When they were asleep, my Ken doll and I would dance the night away.

This family was different from my own, which was just my parents, my older sister, Anika, and me. My father's father had passed away before I was born, and my father's mother, Honey, lived worlds away, in Florida. Aside from occasional phone calls and greeting cards sent back and forth, we didn't really know Honey or anyone else on that side of the family. To me, they were like fictional characters in a book I'd read. I had to imagine what they looked like, how they talked, and what kind of lives they lived on palm-tree-lined streets. Instead, we were close to my mother's parents, Mémère and Pépère—"grandmother" and "grandfather," thanks to our French Canadian roots. My aunt and uncle didn't have kids so there were no first cousins. Our holidays together were warm and intimate but small. Anika and I were always forced to entertain ourselves, and since she was almost seven years older than me, that meant I had to entertain myself. I wanted to know what it would feel like to have a whole house bursting with laughter, songs, and people moving in all directions but still tightly tethered together, like the Huxtables or the Tanners on TV. My family—the one I dreamed about—would be big, boisterous, and *happy*, nestled in the safety and security of a white picket fence around a cozy home.

At that time, home for us was Attleboro, Massachusetts, a small, predominantly White town about forty miles south of Boston, once known as the Jewelry Capital of the World because of all their jewelry manufacturing companies. By the time we arrived in 1988, I didn't see much jewelry, just remnants of the industrial revolution—massive, rusting, empty factories and mills and crowded worker housing that stood in their shadows. Those edifices became as familiar to me as hockey games, warm cider, gray winter days, snow boots left to melt at the front door, clambakes in the summer, and the smell of burning leaves in the fall.

My parents found a single-family home on a long, wooded street just a couple of miles away from the city's dump because it was affordable and provided a manageable commute into Boston for my father. My sister and I made friends soon enough through school, ballet classes, and a family or two in the neighborhood. But Attleboro was different from the more diverse town of Newton, Massachusetts, that we left behind. In Attleboro, *we* were different. Not just because we were a part of the meager 3 percent of Black families that lived there,[2] but also because our family was a coming together of Black and White, and that was something that didn't happen. Races coming together.

When I wasn't dreaming in the car, I'd look up through the window and watch the tops of trees and white clouds dance by in alternating rhythms. If it was nighttime, the treetops looked like black arms and hands outstretched toward a pink-orange or violet-blue sky. I convinced myself that the fingertips were reaching for something—something they knew was there, just a bit higher. They didn't have to see it. They just believed. I knew what it felt like to not see something but still know it was there. Every day, I was reaching too. I had this feeling in my little stomach and chest beating to get out, and with it, a faint whisper telling me that I might have something special to offer the world. Promise. Potential. Ability. My fingers were open, waiting, but they couldn't wrap around it just yet.

Every now and then, my eyes would wander to the front seat to see if my parents' conversation had turned into a fight—one usually erupted every couple of days. I knew the signs, and they were the same no matter where we were, whether in the car or at home. My dad's free hand waving back and forth and his voice getting so loud I squinted my eyes to brace myself because it felt like something was about to snap—the spoon in my hand, the hands on the wall clock, the whole house right into two pieces. And my mother, she would nod her head, her mouth shaped into that familiar frown. There wasn't much I could do then but cry. Or sometimes, if I could block it out, I'd just wrap myself up in my own world again. I'd squeeze my eyes shut and say the Lord's Prayer, hoping he'd hear it and make the fighting stop.

· · · · ·

For the first nineteen years of my life, I wasn't anyone's mother. I was just Nicole, a smart-mouthed, strong-willed, star-gazing kid, born in Stamford, Connecticut, on a Wednesday night in March 1980 after my mom dropped my sister off at a birthday party. My mother says I was doing push-ups on a towel at the pool in our apartment complex at just a few weeks old, and this sounds about right. I was never content with staying put. My curiosity about the world made the cold, snowy New England days that consumed the first half of my childhood and kept me confined to the house absolute torture. The silent, thick blanket of white constantly stretched across our one-level, gray rancher, our yard, the woods across the street, and the few other houses I could see from my bedroom window, sealing us safely inside.

I passed the time cooking with my mother in our kitchen surrounded by the 1970s green-and-pink flowered wallpaper she always vowed to take down but never did. She would drape an apron over me and tie it around my back as we talked through the ingredients for the chocolate chip cookies or pecan pie we would soon place in the warm oven. I watched her closely, taking mental notes of how to hold the bowl, scrape the sides so as to mix all of the ingredients, and follow the recipe precisely. If we made mistakes, we laughed until our faces hurt. Sometimes she would indulge me while I talked to an imaginary camera in the corner of the kitchen as the host of my own cooking show. She, of course, was my sous-chef, handing me utensils and ingredients as I called for them. At the end, as a reward, she would let me lick the spoon.

My other amusements included drawing, reading, singing, playing with my dolls, and most of all, writing. My pen was my ship, and any paper or napkins I could find around the house served as the limitless ocean. This was my escape. I wrote poems about the ways the seasons change, how anger feels when it stays bottled up inside, and what I imagined falling in love was like. I wrote whole chapter books about a group of teenage girlfriends and their adventures—adventures I wished I would one day have. Boys. Shopping. School dances. Perfect families. Parents who never fought, or parents who were divorced. Never parents who stayed together and argued constantly.

Anika and I got used to the yelling and the crying. Soon, it stifled the laughter. Our childhoods were built around it, as if it was another member of the family. It determined whether our friends could come over to play or whether we could watch a television show without being worried about what was going on in the next room. At a very young age, I knew how to worry. The look on my mom's face after a fight was enough to make me wonder if my parents were getting a divorce or if I was to blame for things that I was too young to even understand. But whenever she caught my little eyes staring at her, she would sniffle away her sadness and force a smile.

I never saw anything physical, but the words sliced right through me. Anika and I were always afraid to stick up for each other because we thought the anger might then be directed at us. We were never able to fully rely on any bit of happiness because we had to be ready for what seemed like a normal discussion to bubble over and become an all-consuming roar, for hours. When that happened, as a little girl, I'd sit outside of their door, frozen, hugging my knees to my chest. Or I'd find ways to discreetly slip my mother little notes of comfort scribbled on torn pieces of paper: "Don't cry." "I love you, Mommy." "You're beauti-ful. Smile." As Anika and I got older, though, the fighting drowned out everything else, and we just yearned for the day that we could cast out on our own, away from home and away from the pain.

But there were also parts of my life that I loved. Like the way my fa-ther's jazz made our house come alive every night. Or lazy Sundays after church, watching movies in my pajamas in the room I shared with An-ika. Or how my parents always engaged us in intellectual conversations about politics or race, never dismissing us as too young to understand. Or barbecue dinners outside on our deck while the summer sunset painted orange, pink, and purple hues around us. Or racing in the car to Emerald Square Mall with my dad to get Mrs. Fields ooey-gooey chocolate chip cookies right before it closed. Or how much my family *loved to laugh* and how, every now and then, my father would swing my mother around in the kitchen and dance to Aretha Franklin's "Freeway of Love." And even though we lived modestly, there was always food in the fridge, a roof over our heads, and gifts under the Christmas tree. My parents were both there in my life, both college graduates, and both working in fields they were passionate about. These things would be central to who I would become.

More than twenty years later, I would meet young people with situa-tions far worse than mine. They had survived traumatic and heartbreak-ing childhoods that were difficult to comprehend. Young people who suffered physical or sexual abuse at the hands of their mother or father or someone else they trusted and loved. Young people who were raped, sometimes once, sometimes many times, by a man ten or fifteen years older who claimed to love them. Young people who came to this country as toddlers, traumatized by the experience of crossing the border and being separated from their parents. Young people who grew up homeless, hungry, and in extreme poverty, moving from shelter to shelter, or couch to couch. Young people who had to endure more than just a few months with a drug addict like Stacey. Every day, forced to fend for themselves, they came home from school to a parent who was sprawled across their kitchen or bathroom floor. Young people who never really had parents at all, having lived most of their lives in foster care or having lost a mother or father to death or incarceration. And I would meet others who, like me, grew up with fractured, tenuous relationships with their families because of conflict or divorce or estrangement.

One common theme woven throughout all of our experiences is that, despite what people assume, our pregnancies were not the first thing to ever happen to us. Like a broken necklace, the pregnancy was not the first bead to have fallen. Another had fallen long before, and when it fell, each thing thereafter seemed to inevitably slip off the straight path that was supposed to be the trajectory of our lives.

My friend Reginald, motivated by the teen pregnancies of his mother and three of his four sisters, would later join me in my work to remove barriers for teen parents and their children, often says, "We are more than a moment." I would learn that as practitioners, policy makers, and educators, we erroneously build interventions that define young people by a single moment in their lives. This is especially true for teen mothers and fathers. We begin with the pregnancy as the thing that started a cascade of struggles in their lives, ignoring all that came before because it allows us to overlook all the ways we have failed them. But if we begin at the true *beginning*, the pregnancy is no longer the singular issue. It's just a symptom of larger, often systemic, issues. Larger issues in a family. Larger issues in a country.

In our country, teen pregnancy disproportionately affects young people of color. In 2017, the birth rates for Hispanic and Black teens were more than two times higher than the rate for White teens, and the rate for Native teens was the highest of all races and ethnicities.[3] This isn't because White teens have superior decision-making. In fact, in that same year, more babies were born to White teenage girls than to teenage girls of any other race or ethnicity.[4] The lopsided numbers have to do with something much bigger than one teen's choices or decisions. They are the results of centuries of limiting opportunity and freedom for Native Americans, Blacks, Hispanics, and others, beginning with genocide, slavery, and marginalization when the colonists first arrived. These racist policies were woven together to grow a nation by oppressing certain groups of people to keep economic power in the hands of the few, and they continue to make up the very fabric of the systems we operate within today.

While I couldn't see these broader conditions at play in my own life when I was a teen, I see them now in the lives of the students I work with. Students like Chelsea, a devoted mother, talented artist, and junior at Bowie State University. When Chelsea talks about her childhood, the memories come to her like fragmented, blurry images, flashing in and out of focus. Her father physically abusing her mother, couches barricading bedroom doors because of her mother's mental illness, bullying by classmates who didn't understand her shyness, a series of moves from one relative's house to another. In high school, she was sexually assaulted in the school stairwell while waiting for a bus to take her to a swim meet. "The administrators told me I set the guy up, and it was my fault," she said. "It made high school a terrible place for me." Chelsea learned from a young age to keep quiet in the midst of pain, and this was reinforced by the officials at her school after she told them she had been violated. Like so many Black girls, Chelsea was silenced. As Tarana Burke, who founded the Me Too movement in 2006 to center marginalized people in the conversation around sexual violence, said, "This is about how we've been socialized to view Black women and girls. It's internalized and external oppression." All of this before Chelsea even became pregnant.

Some might say that the sexual assault of a young woman in my program and the careless response of the adults who were supposed to protect her had nothing to do with her race, her oppression, or what happened when the first colonists arrived more than four hundred years ago. But, doing this work, I understand that oppression permeates our entire system, creating enduring inequalities in education, discrimination in the workplace, broken families, high incarceration rates, and other hurdles that have kept communities of color in poverty. Native Americans, Blacks, and Hispanics have the highest poverty rates in the US, and poverty is connected to higher rates of sexual assault and rape.[5] In 2017, *FiveThirtyEight* reported on data from the National Crime Victimization Survey, released annually by the Bureau of Justice Statistics, and found that those in poverty are twelve times more likely than others to report being victims of sexual assault or rape. The statistics on sexual assault in communities of color are disturbing. More than half of all Black girls experience sexual abuse by the age of eighteen.[6] Indigenous women are victims of rape and sexual assault at a rate nearly three times higher than any other race.[7] More than 20 percent of all Latinas have experienced sexual assault.[8] This is just one example of how race affects everything. Poverty. Sexual assault. Teen pregnancy. Everything.

Every intervention, every policy decision, every response to a young person in our care, must involve a step back, a scan of the situation to see if we're starting at the *beginning*, and the true beginning always considers race. What was the first bead to fall for Chelsea? Not the pregnancy, and not the sexual assault. Not the brokenness of her family but the brokenness of our country. Here, at the beginning, we can examine all the ways our long-standing policies and systems leave our young people— precious young people like Chelsea—exposed, unprotected, vulnerable, and disenfranchised. We, who craft programs and policies and allocate resources, have mastered the art of avoiding the things that scare us the most because facing those things makes them more real, gives them a credibility that requires *action*.

· · · · ·

As we always knew she would, Anika went off to college, when I was eleven. She was a straight-A student, something that seemed to come to her without much effort. Academically, Anika set the bar at *Perfect*. Perfect handwriting, perfect origami, perfect French pronunciation, perfect calculations on the first try. She cruised through the SATs and wrote poignant college essays that I'm sure made it hard for any admissions counselor to reject her application. I, on the other hand, earned As and Bs, and they did not all come easily. In our house, it was never a question of *whether* Anika and I would go to college but *where* we would go to college. It wasn't because the price tag didn't matter. In fact, it mattered a lot. My parents didn't have the money for tuition. Instead, they pushed us hard academically, hoping scholarships and grants would cover the costs. I see now that their unfettered optimism was the result of going to college at a time when the federal government saw an economic advantage in investing in college affordability with the GI Bill and the National Defense Student Loan program, later the Federal Perkins Loan program. While these supports weren't designed for either of them, as a Black man or a White woman, they instilled a general feeling that if you wanted to go to college, the government would help foot the bill, and college was no longer an experience reserved just for the wealthy elite.

By the time Anika and I went to college, in the 1990s, these investments dropped significantly, intentionally replaced by private lending. At
the same time, tuition costs skyrocketed. The government wasn't in the
business of making higher education more attainable anymore, especially
as the civil rights movement was making it more accessible for people of
color. College was not free or low cost. The challenge for middle-class
and low-income families was now finding a way to make it *possible*. Even
with the high costs, my parents, like many Americans, understood that
college was our best chance at succeeding in life. So, we always knew that
it was the next step after high school. This was not conjecture or theory.
It was fact.

· · · · ·

My parents moved from Attleboro to Virginia Beach, Virginia, in the
middle of my seventh-grade year. My father got a job at Old Dominion
University in Norfolk, the next town over, in its distance learning program, and we followed. There weren't many graphic design companies in
Virginia Beach, so my mom went back to her roots, as an art teacher for
Newport News Public Schools, just over the water. We emptied all of our
belongings into a brown, three-bedroom house in a subdivision called
Lake Christopher that they rented for eight hundred dollars a month,
and then I began the familiar, tiring act of treading water in a new place. I
had to catch up academically so my grades stayed on track. I had to make
friends. Brandon Middle School in Virginia Beach was three times as big
as Peter Thacher Junior High School back in Attleboro. The hallways
seemed like a limitless sea of strangers.

I also had to adapt to what seemed like a foreign world—the South.
Even the landscape was different. Virginia Beach was sunny, lush, green,
and flat. There were miles of sandy beaches with coral-colored hotels
and properties overlooking the vast ocean. Everything seemed so new.
The contemporary homes and apartments were apportioned into sub-
divisions with flowery names like Brigadoon and Emerald Forest. No
rusting, empty factories. No jewelry manufacturers. More like shipyards
and coal piers. The big business there was the military. Hampton Roads,
a group of counties, cities, and towns on the Virginia Peninsula including
Virginia Beach, was home to nine major military installations. I knew

nothing about the military, except that Pépère had served as a radar and communications officer in the Navy during World War II and didn't talk about it much. The sprawling bases were guarded by checkpoints and ominous fences. I would meet so many friends whose lives were intricately connected to and dictated by what happened behind those fences.

In some ways, the South was friendlier than the North. I remember how startled my parents and I were when a woman's voice thick with a Southern drawl rang out over the loudspeaker welcoming us to a gas station when we first arrived in Virginia. That never happened in Massachusetts. There were more people who looked like me in Virginia. At Thacher, I had been one of three Black students in the entire school. At Brandon, almost a third of the students were Black. It was exciting to be around more Brown faces, but it wasn't easy to find community. In Massachusetts, my brown skin made my five-year-old neighbor afraid to touch me, fearing my color would "rub off" on him; it made "nigger" roll off my classmate's tongue with ease. In Virginia, my skin was too light, making some of my Black peers assume I was stuck up or conceited. Turns out, I was different everywhere.

Eventually, I made friends. I even found a short-lived boyfriend, Jean Paul, who was Dominican and obsessed with baseball. Back in Attleboro right before we moved, I had my first kiss with a White boy, Justin. It was a big production outside in front of all of our friends. So, having a boyfriend was somewhat of a new phenomenon. Jean Paul and I mostly walked to class holding hands and talked on the phone. I made honor roll, which both impressed and annoyed my teachers since I talked too much in class and rolled my eyes when they reprimanded me for it. I joined a service club called the Busy Bees that met after school and took us to nearby nursing homes to do arts and crafts activities with senior citizens. By June, I liked Virginia Beach, even liked it better than Attleboro.

· · · · ·

Every now and then, a pretty girl stared back at me in the mirror. The seventeen-year-old boys hollered at me out of car windows when I walked down the long stretch of Kempsville Road to get home from school. They saw flowing, curly black hair and light brown skin, full lips, and shapely legs. But most of the time, I saw a little girl who licked cookie batter off of too many spoons, still popped in a retainer at night, and could have worn nicer clothes.

After Jean Paul, I dated a series of Black boys. There was another Justin, my middle school on-and-off boyfriend. He was smart, made me laugh, and would do just about anything for me, it seemed. I broke up with him just before Valentine's Day in eighth grade, and he had a lavish bouquet and a teddy bear delivered to my classroom in an effort to win me back. The flower arrangement was so big, the teacher thought it was for her. In ninth grade, I dated a sweet, quiet boy named Alex for two months, then broke up with him because I thought his grades were too low. Then I dated Shawn, who was two years older than me and went to Salem High School, about twenty minutes away. I was mostly enamored by the fact that he sang in an aspiring R&B group, and he and the other members wore big diamond earrings and all-black outfits like Jodeci, including black leather jackets and aviator sunglasses. I broke up with him after I found out he was cheating. Boys and romance were fine, but I had bigger plans.

My first article was published at age eleven—a piece on growing up biracial—in a printed newsletter called *The Interracial Family Alliance*. When the payment of ten dollars came in the mail as a check, I told my mom I never wanted to spend it and tacked it on my wall as a daily reminder of what I was working toward. My passion for writing advanced from filling napkins and notebooks around the house with my poems and stories to writing about real issues as a high school correspondent for the regional *Virginian-Pilot* newspaper. I pursued the most controversial topics—things that affected me directly. My articles on affirmative action policies and the media's influence on young girls' body images appeared on the front page of the features section. Denise and Laura, the adult reporters who ran the high school correspondent program, were surprised but impressed by my desire to write about such complex subjects. I liked the idea of using words to change the way people thought about things, and when I saw how proud my dad was to open the newspaper and see my name in print, I was hooked. Journalism was my calling.

In the *Pilot* newsroom after school one day, Laura sat on the corner of her desk while reporters buzzed behind her and told me that the University of Maryland had one of the best journalism programs in the country.

Without ever even seeing the campus, I made it my top college choice. Anika's attempts to persuade me otherwise—she'd gone to a small public school in Virginia called the College of William & Mary—could not change my mind. I didn't care how big the university was or whether it was out-of-state. I didn't pause to think about what my experience would be like at a predominantly White institution like the University of Maryland. I just knew it was my ticket to becoming a successful journalist, like Laura and Denise, and my ticket to leaving home. Most of my friends were saving their college research and decisions for senior year, but I had a concrete plan. I was on my way.

. . . . .

When I met him—even the very first time I saw him—I wanted to know more about him. I was drawn to him. His skin was ebony silk, the kind you wanted to feel underneath your fingertips. His rich black hair was cut close to his head, and then later, he grew it into dreads that he'd twist between his fingers when he slumped down in his chair in class. He had an athletic build. Not too big, not too small, but a perfectly proportioned, muscular physique. Tattoos on both arms. He entered a room with a carefree, agile stride, full laugh, and palpable charisma. He had a bright, boyish smile—much different from the grown-up things he'd been through. His smile made happiness grow roots inside of your soul. It was contagious.

But what attracted me from the very first glance were his eyes. Deep, dark brown with hollows around them. They had a story to tell. My daughter has the same eyes.

I first saw him in seventh grade shortly after arriving at Brandon. I was walking down the hallway hidden in the shell of my bulky black coat. Somehow, in the waves of heads bobbing along in front of me, I noticed him strolling in the opposite direction. He stood out from the humdrum of the crowd, the schedule, and the routine around us. There was a different rhythm to the way he moved, a nonchalant boldness that seemed years ahead of the rest of us. He was free. Free from the bell that was about to ring and the teachers who patrolled the hallway. It was as if he could step outside into the early afternoon sunshine at any moment and keep going.

As he came closer, his eyes found me. We locked in on each other, holding our connection for a few seconds too long. Then he flashed a warm, playful smile as if he knew everything I was thinking and wondering. A rush of red hot spread across my face, and I looked away before slipping into my classroom, where I found my seat and tried to shake the feeling that he had stolen the air right from my lungs. Not long after I learned his name, he disappeared. He spent the next two years at the city's alternative high school for selling weed.

His name was Rakheim.

We wouldn't see each other again until our freshman year at Tallwood High School. I was once again nervous, disoriented, and, this time, overwhelmed by just the thought of high school. I was jiggling the lock on my blue metal locker after having tried the combination three times. I glanced over my shoulder to see if anyone was witnessing my struggle and found him. He was making his way down the hallway with the same assurance as before but even more maturity. His dreads were now a couple of inches long. He was dressed head to toe in expensive clothes, a navy blue-and-white Nautica sweatshirt, Pepe Jeans, and pristine Air Jordans. He didn't carry himself like a freshman. Instead, it was as if he owned the building and everyone in it. Guys shouted his name down the hallway, and girls stopped to give him hugs. He even joked around with a couple of the football coaches.

His eyes found me. He flashed his bright smile and this time, nodded his head, recognizing me from our days at Brandon. It felt as if we were back in seventh grade in that yellow sterile hallway in a crowd of people yet somehow just the two of us. My cheeks burned, and I fixed my eyes on the stubborn lock to pull myself back together. After he passed, I turned around and watched him embrace a very pretty senior. Monique. His girlfriend. He threw his arm around her and walked with her down the hall.

It wasn't until tenth grade that he became more than just a mysterious, magnetic force. When I walked into my health class for the first time and saw him sitting there patting the seat behind him, I pretended to be annoyed. I rolled my eyes when he turned around and whispered, "Hey, baby," even though my stomach did a flip.

Rakheim was the first guy that I talked to about more than just baseball or school. We shared real problems and emotions and worries.

When he came to class stinking like weed, I'd try to convince him to stop smoking so much. When I told him about all the things I'd heard about my boyfriend Shawn, he'd try to tell me that they were true, that he was indeed cheating. Rakheim was failing most of his classes, and I'd urge him to take school more seriously. He also whispered different kinds of sexual positions in my ear, which I'd wave away. We talked about the rumors too. People said he sold drugs, not just weed. He always wore chunky gold chains, pricey clothes, and the newest sneakers. He said the rumors were mostly untrue. Yes, he sold weed sometimes, but it was just for some spending money. His older brother bought most of his clothes.

We shared our ambitions. I was going to be a serious journalist, traveling from country to country, solving the world's most pressing problems with my pen and notepad. He loved the thought of that, and he had his own grandiose, extravagant dreams: the NFL. Mansions. Cars. When he talked about them, he was giddy and so confident about himself and his future in football that I thought nothing could penetrate that. It was exciting and intoxicating and so different from the life I lived. He painted a picture of those two visions coming together, a professional running back married to a Pulitzer Prize–winning writer. He wanted to be my tall, dark, and handsome, and even though that didn't seem likely, when he rubbed his finger down the length of my pinky, my skin came alive. It was worth letting him believe it just to feel rebellion rushing through my veins.

. . . . .

I squinted against the afternoon sunlight in Jay's Wings, a favorite hole-in-the-wall spot about three minutes away from Tallwood. My friend Bree and I often went to Jay's after school to reflect on the day before heading home for studying and parents and everything else. The Blockbuster video store next door made it difficult to find parking, but the food was good. Fried everything. You could smell the oil in the air.

We came to Jay's that day to think through a dilemma. I had broken up with Shawn, and the junior prom was only two months away. All of the potential dates had been scooped up. I was dateless.

I'd been thinking about someone in particular for a while but hadn't gotten up the nerve to say his name. I was worried about her reaction—worried about *everyone's* reaction. Bree was always so quick to judge. Rakheim was someone you never took seriously, and I was struggling with what it would really mean to ask him to prom. Would it just be a date? Or would I be inviting something more into my life? And if it was more, Rakheim wasn't the type to just trickle in. He would come crashing at me with an all-consuming flood of intensity. That's what it would mean to love him.

"What about Rakheim?" I blurted out.

Her eyes got wide, and she smiled. "Yes! Nicole, that would be too cute!"

. . . . .

When I was fourteen, I found gospel music on a purple flyer in the hallway announcing auditions for Tallwood's choir. I stared at it for a few minutes. My mom and I had stopped going to the Catholic church on Kempsville Road around the corner from our house a year earlier because it seemed to fit less and less into our busy schedules. My relationship with God and religion had been molded in Attleboro by regular weekly sessions of Confraternity of Christian Doctrine (CCD) and consistent Sunday services at Saint John the Evangelist Church on Main Street. Now, in Virginia, I felt disconnected and interrupted. The choir would be an opportunity for me to worship with others again. I ripped one of the tiny slips with the day and time for the auditions from the bottom of the flyer: Tuesday at 2:45 p.m.

The majority of people in the choir were Baptist, mostly girls, all Black. Being raised in the Catholic Church, my mother's faith, meant these hymns were foreign to me. They were rooted in sacred Black oral traditions handed down from generation to generation. I had to learn the hand clapping, foot stomping, and rhythmic sway to the music, but it didn't take long. Soon it felt natural, intrinsic. Gospel music, like so many aspects of Black culture that I'd been introduced to in those five years since moving to Virginia, felt as if it had been a latent, undiscovered part of me all along. Like baked macaroni and cheese, slightly browned and bubbling on top. Luster's Pink Oil, relaxers, and silk hair wraps for sleeping. The swagger and style—Cross Colours, Los Angeles rappers in their lowriders, and sagging jeans. Even Rakheim.

The best thing about the choir, the thing that made me fall in love with it, was how we sounded when all of our voices came together. I was a part of something bigger and better than myself. My imperfections didn't matter. We were perfect, together. And when we stepped into the classroom of the choir director, Mrs. Davis, our voices blended together in harmonies that would sometimes make her cry and would at the same time make me feel suddenly inadequate and unworthy.

I looked forward to choir practice. I looked forward to school. I looked forward to almost anything that was a legitimate reason to be away from home. At Tallwood, I held an editorial position at the newspaper and yearbook and designed the cover of the literary magazine, in addition to writing articles for the *Pilot*. I was the regional vice president of Future Educators of America and president of the French Honors Society. I took honors and Advanced Placement classes, burying myself in homework and novels—*Wuthering Heights, Invisible Man, Frankenstein*. On weeknights, I'd get home at about 6 p.m., and on weekends, I was usually performing somewhere with the choir or volunteering.

I loved the sensation of busyness.

The constant state of *doing* distracted me from the things I didn't want to feel or face, the things I couldn't do anything about. My mother's uncanny ability to smile through her pain served as a regular, silent lesson in survival. *Avoid the things that scare you the most.* So I filled the hours with things that I could control, things that felt validating. I turned to school. I turned to clubs, extracurricular activities. I turned to friends. I turned to Rakheim, and I turned to the choir. I counted down the minutes until we'd stand together in two lines—altos, sopranos, and tenors—and make beautiful music. Together.

CHAPTER 2

WOMEN'S WORK

I COULD HEAR A SMILE spread across Rakheim's face when I called to ask him to be my date for the prom. I knew that smile.

"Of course," he said, laughing, and we both knew that we were talking about more than just the prom.

As I suspected, there was no effort involved when it came to my falling for Rakheim or Rakheim falling for me. We had both felt it for a long time. Now everything just fell into place. We talked on the phone a few more times before he asked me out for our first date—a trip to Lynnhaven Mall and then to TCBY for some frozen yogurt.

"You pretty. You know that?" He said sitting across from me at the tiny table, lowering his head and tilting it to the side to catch my glance.

"Shut up," I laughed, and looked back down at my green lime sorbet. My cheeks tingled the way they always did when he was around.

"I'm serious. You know that, though," he said. "When we were in Coach Hudson's class together, I'd always be lookin' at you. Not lookin' at you in the way you think. I'd be like, 'Damn, that girl is pretty.'"

Away from school, teachers, and everyone else, Rakheim was even more intoxicating because his attention was solely focused on me. There were no distractions. I could feel the crushing wave of him rolling over me, and I was struggling just to break the surface to catch my breath.

"Can I kiss you?" His voice sounded so gentle, so different from the loud proclamations that came booming down the hallway, telling everyone Tallwood was going to win the football game that night or commenting on how good some girl looked in her skirt.

I looked up.

His fingers touched my cheek. He leaned forward. His lips were softer than I thought they'd be.

· · · · ·

In the weeks leading up to prom, there was nothing else to talk about but preparing for the night. Every conversation at lunch, on the phone, and at Jay's Wings involved our dresses, to ensure no one was wearing anything too similar, predictions of how the night would unfold, or ironing out the evening's logistics. Tickets. Transportation. Timing. Dinner beforehand. A plan for group pictures at the photo booth. The after-party.

Teachers and school administrators meanwhile were pushing safety messages. They scheduled several D.A.R.E. presentations, involving local police officers coming into classrooms as part of the "Just Say No" to drugs program. I don't remember much about their visits except the briefcase of drug paraphernalia they left open on the table and the stern demeanor of the officers, who usually wore all black uniforms with shorts and guns holstered on their hips. Five years later, the US surgeon general would issue a statement on the ineffectiveness of the Drug Abuse Resistance Education program, saying, "Children who participate are as likely to use drugs as those who do not participate." This won't surprise me. Like so many people working in rigid prevention programs—whether sex or drugs—the officers never asked us questions about our experiences, our lives, or our feelings. They barely cracked a smile.

What left more of an impression on me was the mock car crash that was displayed on the lawn of the school for several weeks leading up to prom. The twisted and distorted metal made me cringe each time I pulled my parents' station wagon into the parking lot—maybe because I knew how fast Rakheim liked to drive.

Now, as we sat around the table with all of the other couples, he was a perfect gentleman. He opened doors for me, pulled out my chair, asked me if I needed anything. Bree smiled in amazement from across the table. It almost made you forget this was the same Rakheim who was known to be promiscuous, juggling multiple girls at a time. The same Rakheim who dabbled in drug dealing, disappeared all the time, fought on—and off—the football field, and had a reputation for being kind of dangerous. It was evidence enough for me to believe that somehow in the couple of months that we'd been dating, I'd succeeded in changing him, in making him more caring and responsible and committed. Miraculously, I was all he needed.

After dinner, we leisurely headed toward the car, only to see from a distance that it was being towed. Rakheim had insisted on parking close to the restaurant and had blocked someone's driveway. We ran hand in hand across the street to the tow truck, and Rakheim talked a short man with long dreads and a grease-stained T-shirt that barely covered the bottom of his protruding belly into unhooking the car. He explained to him that the car was his stepsister's brand-new Neon, and Tina would kill him if we didn't bring it back to her on time. Plus, he said, it was my prom night. The man looked us up and down for a minute before grinning and shaking his head. Rakheim could talk his way out of anything. He'd paint a sad picture, bum a Newport off of the person, and soon they'd forget all about the dispute. It was sort of magical to watch.

As we drove, Rakheim lowered the volume only slightly to make a few calls on Tina's cell phone while I watched incredulously. It was impressive just to have a pager, let alone a cell phone. When he wasn't on the phone, he was smoking a blunt, blowing the smoke into the night air.

The Marriott downtown had a long lobby lined with huge windows adorned with lush red curtains that hung from the ceiling to the red and gold carpeted floor. As we walked down the grandiose corridor with our hands woven together, I could feel everyone's eyes on us as if we were on a fashion runway, being critiqued and assessed from head to toe. Most people hadn't seen Rakheim—the star football player—since he disappeared from Tallwood, and they certainly hadn't expected him to show up at the prom, never mind with me.

But I liked the attention that followed him wherever he went. Either you knew him, knew of him, or wanted to know him. No one really challenged Rakheim because he had made a name for himself. As his girlfriend, I liked that I was attached to that name and attached to what I thought was its protection, safety, and security. He never shied away from a fight. He seemed to relish any opportunity to defend his friends and his neighborhood, College Park. The seven of them—him, his friends, and a cousin—were inseparable, like brothers. You could always find them together in some combination. When they went to parties, they showed up in a big group, already drunk or high, ready to tear the place up because of a rivalry with another school or neighborhood. I didn't understand at the time, and neither did Rakheim, but their tight-knit group, similar to my vision for a big happy family, was a substitute for the stable families they didn't have.

As the night went on, we mingled, finding each other every now and then. People were eager to talk to him, asking him about his new school, I.C. Norcom, in Portsmouth where he was now living with his older sister, Paula, and her family, and praising him for rushing for 720 yards and twelve touchdowns in the regular season during his first year there. Bree and I danced to Missy Elliott, Aaliyah, and Mariah Carey, singing at the top of our lungs, and taking breaks by the punch bowl to people watch. But when "Un-Break My Heart" by Toni Braxton came on, I searched for him in the crowd while people coupled together around me, swaying back and forth to the ballad.

"Have you seen Rakheim?" I asked a girl I knew from the choir.

"I think he's out there, dancing," she said pointing in the direction of the dance floor.

And he was. His arms were wrapped around Denise, a girl whom he'd had sex with several times—and in several classrooms—before he left Tallwood. Everyone knew it. Rumors swirled around the school about it for weeks until whispers about his disappearance, and then the death of his mother, took their place. My face was hot and stinging, and the sensation soon spread to my chest, arms, and legs. My hands, heavy at my sides, began to shake. I balled them up into tight fists. I didn't feel so pretty anymore.

· · · · ·

Twenty years later, my daughter will keep a stack of photographs in her closet. They will be a collection of images of her dad, some that I will set aside for her, and some that he will give her over the years. A photo of her sitting between his legs in the wet sand at Huntington Park Beach in Newport News one summer afternoon when she is three years old.

Another of the two of them lounging on the roof of a car in the parking lot of a friend's apartment complex when she is eight, missing a tooth. Somewhere in the stack, there will be a photo of him and me in the foyer of my parents' house in Virginia Beach. Me with a tall ponytail of cascading spiral curls, pink lip gloss, a gold shawl, and a long olive-green dress. Him in a black tuxedo, spiky dreads pulled back from his face with a rubber band, and his hand resting on my hip. Both of us brimming with excitement, seeming irreversibly in love.

The glossy picture is the only evidence she will have that her parents were ever really together and that they ever loved each other. This will be hard for her to imagine without the photograph, not only because the relationship will end before she can even remember it but also because we will be so different by the time she is a teenager—because *I* will be so different from that young girl smiling into the camera. Frustrated by the photo's inability to answer her questions, she will ask me how I even started dating her dad, and I'll struggle to explain it.

I was smart. I had a clear vision for what I wanted my future to look like. I had a carefully charted, color-coded path in my carefully marked-up planner to get there. The dangers of dating Rakheim should have been clear. But when I was in high school, there was no such thing as healthy or unhealthy love. I just knew *love*, and that love was turbulent and chaotic and painful, and it held on no matter how ugly things got. It took my breath away in a middle-school hallway and gave me goose bumps with just a slight pinky touch. Sometimes it yelled at me, threatened me, betrayed me, and even hurt me. Like a wave, it sucked me into its undertow, as opposed to me choosing whether or not it was worthy of my heart. I had no concept of gauging its health, asking questions, or making assessments. I had no concept of deserving more. I was simply its prey.

Years later, most of the relationships that the young parents in my program find themselves in will have the same origins. There will be very little intentionality around their dating decisions, no sense of filtering people out by qualities or character, and few examples of healthy relationships to look to. In 2009, ChildTrends will release a report saying, "The scarcity of models of healthy adult relationships seriously hinders the ability of both teen girls and teen boys to forge such relationships themselves." Left with little guidance, most stumble into relationships in the midst of a whirlwind or at a vulnerable time in their lives, as I did, barely having the capacity or the vocabulary to ask themselves if someone is a good person. And sometimes, a young person can be so desperate for someone to latch onto in the storm that everything is secondary to just needing to be anchored in something—in anyone. What we talk about most is arming teens with information, teaching them how to identify what's healthy and what's not. That's vitally important, particularly because they often don't see enough healthy relationships. Equally important and less talked about is the need to address the storms that are raging in their lives and robbing them of their power to make decisions. It's like giving someone a Band-Aid for a gunshot wound. For my students, poverty, mental health issues, drug- or alcohol-addicted parents, sexual abuse, scant family support, and more—were all cyclones spinning out of control in their lives before their pregnancies, depriving them of the peace we all need to be fully aware that we even have a choice in who to love.

Once young people are in a toxic relationship, the ties are difficult to sever. Once a child is involved, those ties are nearly impossible to untangle. Girls abused by their boyfriends are more likely to become pregnant, and perhaps unsurprisingly, teen mothers experience higher rates of abuse than their peers.[1] Nearly a quarter of young mothers experience physical or sexual abuse during their pregnancy.[2]

When Chelsea told me her boyfriend became violent not long after he found out she was pregnant, I asked her what made her stay. She said, "I was using him as a safe haven. My family disowned me. I felt isolated. So spending time with him was a way to not think about it. When he became abusive, I didn't feel there was anything I could do about it." We stay because instability, loneliness, and desperation can convince us that we have no other choice and that leaving would be more harmful. We stay because at least we have *someone*. We stay because we're just trying to stop the bleeding.

This will be hard to explain to my daughter. All of it. The storm, the powerlessness I felt, and the things I never want her to know about her dad.

· · · · ·

"You hurt me," I said, back in the car, my voice shaking. "Do you know how it felt to see you dancing out there with *her?*" I held back tears. "I would never do anything like that to you."

This feeling was foreign and confusing. In the past, with other guys, if something didn't feel right, I just walked away. But with Rakheim, I couldn't walk away. It was as if there was something binding us together, a pull or a force that began twisting and forming years before during our first glance at Brandon and became stronger with every interaction after that. Now it was so absolute, just the thought of breaking up with Rakheim was painful. And yet, at the same time, I knew that I had built him up to be something he wasn't. He wasn't faithful. He wasn't a gentleman. He wasn't changed. He was the same person he'd always been. I'd just made excuses because he was with *me* this time, and because I wanted to believe that no matter how different we were, the connection we had would make it work.

And there was his magic. Just hearing him say that his heart was in my hands sent a warmth through my entire body. Those words were all I needed. They convinced me to tuck away any doubts I might have had about his loyalty or his genuineness. They pieced together a picture of the two of us, years in the future, looking back and laughing at a silly misunderstanding on my prom night. I figured I had to teach Rakheim how to love because he had done it so wrong for so long. He didn't have a mother and father to show him. So it wasn't all his fault. He was essentially on his own, and he was my responsibility now. He'd chosen me. Out of all the girls he'd been with and mistreated—out of all the girls who wanted him—Rakheim chose *me* to love. He needed me. We needed each other.

That night, I gave myself to him because I wasn't an awkward chubby little girl when I was with Rakheim. I was a young woman who belonged to someone special. Someone who promised to protect me and love me always. This last wave was the most crushing of all. I was completely submerged, wholly enveloped by him, and I only caught a glimmer of the moonlight dancing on the surface above before completely letting go.

CHAPTER 3

LOVE SONG

A GOSPEL SONG, sung in perfect harmony, is a promise of hope. For some, it affirms that there is an open door, waiting at the end of a lingering dark tunnel. For others, it is a reminder that sunshine always follows an expected or unexpected downpour—that every monsoon runs its course, and then it, too, shall pass. Hymns serenade our soul, igniting our emotions and easing our fears. At seventeen, I was unaware of their full power, but each time our voices rose in unison, the precision and completeness was, for me, an anointing.

We stood in two even rows behind the small altar of a cramped storefront church with our choir director, Mrs. Davis, as always close by. Our freshly ironed white blouses and handmade violet skirts matched the purple and gold scarves draped around our necks. Our eyes followed the young pastor pacing back and forth on the tiny stage, chanting his emotional sermon, while the congregation spontaneously responded with verbal and nonverbal affirmations—"Yes, Lord," "Have mercy," "Jesus," "Alright, now." As synchronized and pristine as we looked positioned behind him, most of us weren't excited to be there.

Ocean View was where my father lived in a small apartment when he first took the job at Old Dominion before moving the rest of the family down. During our visits to see him, we drove through run-down wooden beach-front properties, boarded-up businesses, and cheap, seedy motels.

It all clashed with the image I had of cheerful couples and families peppering the coast with their large red-and-white beach umbrellas, coolers, funnel cakes, and ice cream. I had no idea that Ocean View was in Norfolk or that its miles of shoreline lacked the tourist attractions, hotels, and elegant beach houses that lined the neighboring Virginia Beach waters.

Before the Hampton Roads Bridge Tunnel and the first section of I-64 opened in 1957 connecting the cities of Norfolk and Virginia Beach with the cities of Hampton and Newport News, Ocean View was a popular vacation spot for sailors and travelers with streetcars, a boardwalk, and even an amusement park, famous for its wooden roller coaster, The Rocket. But the new tunnel and highways made it easy for tourists to pass Ocean View and vacation instead in Virginia Beach. The area was left to decay, overtaken by dense pockets of poverty and low-income residents. Rakheim's older brother settled in Ocean View because of the low rent and clientele, selling drugs and running a fraudulent-check operation out of his tiny apartment.

When I was a little girl, I thought people were given houses, and through some sort of lottery, you either received a big house or a small house. I figured the houses we lived in over the years were assigned to us by some overarching authority tossing small white balls with black numbers on them or folded-up pieces of paper around in a glass bowl somewhere. My parents explained that housing was instead based on what people could afford, but I didn't understand why everyone couldn't *afford* nice housing. Why did one family have the ability to purchase a house too big for them to ever really use and another family only have the ability to rent a tiny apartment with no heat? What did the family in the tiny apartment do wrong? And maybe if we could identify what they did wrong, we could help them fix it. I was frustrated by the unfairness of it and drawn to the people who were most consumed by it—people who mostly looked like me.

As I got older, my confusion about poverty was overpowered by a narrative taught mostly at school and on TV that offered a simple answer. People are poor because of their own bad decisions and their unwillingness to work to achieve the "American Dream." This seemed to make sense. I could look around at my classmates and see that those who were working hard were earning better grades than those who were barely showing up for school. I didn't ask myself *why* those students weren't showing up for school. I didn't ask what kept them away, other than their indifference to learning. There were, of course, legitimate deterrents, like being responsible for younger siblings or excessive disciplinary actions from teachers and administrators. But I didn't try to connect the dots—and no one encouraged me to. My parents didn't promote the rhetoric of individual choices, but they didn't provide a counter to it, most likely because they were still trying to understand it themselves. When we talked about poor people, their faces were heavy with empathy. The conversations focused on our obligation to do something for the less fortunate and to make the world a better place, not on the underlying causes that got them there.

By the time I was in high school, my mentality about people living in poverty was a gumbo of sorts. I was perplexed and heartbroken by the inequities and felt compelled to help. I thought maybe I would go read to little children in that village in Africa one day after all. Or, in the short term, I could volunteer at a soup kitchen or start a fundraiser at school. And while I identified with those who were "othered" and on the fringes because my race was never a simple checkbox, kids made sure I knew I didn't fit in, and home wasn't perfect. I also saw the people living in those boarded-up houses and dilapidated motels in Ocean View—including young mothers, the same age as me, sitting outside watching their children play—as very different. They weren't like *me*. I showed up for school. I worked hard. I made the *right* decisions.

It would be a long time before I was pushed to look beyond the surface, easy explanations for why people are living in poverty and face the structural and institutional barriers that largely dictate their options and predetermine their outcomes. It would be a long time before, at my own nonprofit, my staff and I would ask candidates to answer the question, "Why are people poor?" during our hiring process. If their responses did not reflect an understanding of the systemic causes, including institutional racism, we wouldn't hire them. Putting someone who saw the individual as the sole driver of their circumstances on the front lines with our students—all teen mothers and fathers and 90 percent of them students of color—was both irresponsible and detrimental, we would determine. But this growth and understanding would take years.

Mrs. Davis had little patience for a bunch of kids from the suburbs being turned off by a tiny church in a run-down area. Unlike us, she knew that storefront churches were characteristic of historically Black communities and offered a lifeline to congregants and a stimulant for change in poor neighborhoods. Storefront churches were deeply connected to the people, often fundraising to assist members in times of crisis, stocking pantries to combat the food deserts where they were usually located, and caring for sick residents who couldn't afford medical care. They sometimes offered more than larger, more affluent congregations.

When she heard us snickering because someone said the church used to be a 7-Eleven, the ubiquitous convenience store, she threw us a biting look from the pew she sat in. We straightened our backs and swallowed our giggles. She would be the first Black woman I would come to have a close relationship with—the first to model "Black Girl Magic" for me and the first to also unapologetically show me that we Black women are not superhuman. She was a tiny round ball of energy with a mischievous smile and a stubbornness that often paid off. Despite pushback from teachers and parents who felt a public-school gospel choir violated the separation of church and state from the First Amendment to the US Constitution, Mrs. Davis used her gentle persistence and charm to get her funding approved and keep the choir going each year.

Tonight she expected nothing less than the stellar performance that we would surely have given if we had been singing at the National Cathedral or the Kennedy Center—one full of passion and sincerity. She didn't care what the building looked like. As long as it was a house of God, we belonged there. So on this Saturday evening, we packed into the little church to receive and deliver a bit of hope.

· · · · ·

Rakheim's phone calls became less and less frequent—barely once a week—after prom. I'd call Paula's house in Portsmouth, and in a sad voice, she'd tell me he wasn't home. Each time, I knew she wanted to say more. It was that unspoken language between women, a fluency acquired after years of nursing our own heart wounds and watching them fade to scars. She knew how hopeless this was. She wanted to tell me to stop calling, to move on, and to try to piece my heart back together again. But she didn't, and I wouldn't have listened anyway. So this was the cycle. Me always calling. Someone on the other end always telling me he wasn't there. And because he was at Norcom, and I was at Tallwood, I only saw him when we could set up a meeting at Tina's apartment, which was around the corner from Lake Christopher. During those rare visits, we'd watch some TV and then go into her bedroom. No more dates. No more frozen yogurt. No more dinners at fancy restaurants in Ghent. I took whatever I could get, and he was so sweet and gentle when we were together, it made my anger and frustration seem silly and unwarranted. His voice would be so quiet in my ear. His strong tattooed arms would wrap tightly around my back.

Rakheim was the only one out of his group of friends who had anything productive to do during the long summer days. When he wasn't in Tina's apartment smoking weed with his friends, he was practicing in the hot sun on Norcom's football field. His brother-in-law, who was an assistant coach there, made sure he didn't miss a practice. The others, though, spent their days like this or in summer school making up a failed class. They had hitched their futures to Rakheim's NFL career, thinking he'd bring them along as his entourage, with more women, weed, and money than they could count. We were approaching our last year of high school, but it was clear they had no plans for what was next, and some wouldn't even graduate. They were living day to day.

At the time, I blamed it on a lack of motivation, but now I understand how hard it is to be motivated when opportunities and resources are nearly nonexistent and when the world sees you as a "super-predator," a term coined by John DiIulio Jr., a political science professor at Princeton, when all of us were just beginning high school. DiIulio proposed that "super-predators" had inherently violent natures, with a desire to "kill, rape, maim, and steal without remorse." He also said, without evidence, there were more "super-predators" among the Black population, which both accounted for and justified their higher rates of incarceration. These theories, and others like it, were adopted by politicians, the media, and the larger public, including the Black community, to justify legislation that quietly targeted young Black men, or "thugs." College, good jobs, and stability probably seemed unattainable and futile in the face of this targeting. Having to constantly defend themselves against these labels had to be both frustrating and debilitating.

Rakheim always told me he expected to die young. It was hard for him and his friends to talk about the future beyond the next few days or months. Without seeing the data that Black men have the lowest life expectancy of any major demographic group in the US,[1] they intrinsically knew that they might go to jail or die before realizing their full potential or earning their first gray hairs. They didn't need a study to tell them homicide was, and is, the leading cause of death for Black males under the age of forty-four.[2] They could feel it in their bones as they sat through the funerals of their lost friends or family members. Years later, this will be confirmed by one of my students, Joseph, who grew up in Southeast DC, the poorest part of the city, and became a father at seventeen: "My whole reason for thinking about becoming a parent was due to my environment. I thought I'd be killed, and if I died, I'd have nothing behind my name. I wanted to have a piece of me left behind."

Knowing some of these hazards, I was more inclined to make concessions and excuses for Rakheim. I didn't push for too much information. I didn't ask a lot of questions about where he'd been or what he'd been doing. I didn't want to add any more pressure, or worse, ruin the scarce time we had together. When I finally did muster the courage to ask him why I didn't hear from him like I used to, he told me it was because he was so busy with summer workouts. Much later, he admitted that the "newness" of me had worn off.

Using a practice I'd perfected over the years, I drowned my heartache in a packed schedule, strategically filling the summer with experiences that would make my resume irresistible to the college admissions officers who would soon be reviewing it. Because I wrote for the *Pilot* and Tallwood's newspaper, I was invited to participate in the City of Virginia Beach's week-long youth journalism conference at one of the local high schools. The letter arrived in a pile on the kitchen counter shortly after the prom. I read it over and over, excited about the opportunity to be recognized for my writing and increasing my chances of getting into Maryland's journalism program. Throughout the week, the instructors were impressed with my articles, op-eds, and profiles on various topics and people. I heard a group of them talking about my work during a break one day, noting my "mature voice."

I wanted to share all of this with Rakheim. It was the kind of thing that would make his face light up like it did during our talks about Pulitzer Prizes and Super Bowl rings back at Tallwood, but he wasn't returning my calls. It made the two first-place writing awards that I won that week feel a little less important.

While there are some common characteristics among young parents and certain communities that are disproportionately impacted by teen pregnancy, teen parents are not a monolith. Still, "teen mother" typically conjures up an image of a poor Black girl lacking ambition and drive and determined to take advantage of "the system"—a picture of the "welfare queen" that Ronald Reagan constantly referenced on the 1976 presidential campaign trail. The only quality I shared with this inaccurate, prejudicial stereotype was the color of my skin. I was full of ambition and drive, a middle-class, honor-roll student, college bound, and didn't have any concept of "the system," but like nearly all of the teen mothers and fathers with varying experiences I will come to meet over the years, I had a hole in my heart from years of needing to feel safe and loved. These needs are powerful and persuasive. For me, they took precedence over everything else and compromised nearly every decision I made, from staying in a tortuous relationship to having sex to not using condoms.

Later, in college, I will learn about Abraham Maslow, an American psychologist who created a theory about human needs and the order in which those needs must be met for someone to feel fulfilled and realize their full potential. Maslow's theory will help me better understand why I was willing to put everything on the line for my relationship with Rakheim and why young people with varied backgrounds might experience a pregnancy. The first set of needs in the hierarchy are primary and physiological—air, sleep, water, food, and shelter. Before we can focus on anything else, these requirements must be addressed. The next set center on our safety—the security of our body, family, employment or schooling, resources, and so on—and comprise all of the things needed to protect the body's first set of physiological needs. When we feel secure, we can turn our attention to the next set of needs, which are about love—friendships, family, and intimate relationships. In order to reach the last two levels of esteem and self-actualization, we must first feel loved.

Regardless of my intelligence, or my parents' ability to meet my basic needs, as a teenager, I was overwhelmed and interrupted by wanting to feel safe and loved. Other young women who became pregnant in worse situations than mine were halted at the very first level, raised in homes where food was scarce and eviction was constant—deficiencies that disproportionately plague communities of color. Yet, those around them wondered why they weren't more focused in school or willing to participate in extracurricular activities. If you ask a current or former young mother or father from various walks of life whether each level of their needs on Maslow's hierarchy were met before the pregnancy, their answer is likely "no." My approach to social justice will be highly influenced by this theory and what it tells us about our shared human experience, our basic universal needs, and the imperative of caring for the whole person.

When Rakheim started calling again, it felt as if maybe that hole was shrinking. We became inseparable, falling into the habit of calling each other every morning before school and going again on dates to the movies and the mall. At night, I'd curl up in my bed with the phone to my ear, and we'd talk until morning stood outside our windows and poured light inside. Sometimes, when a phone call wasn't enough, we'd sneak out in the middle of the night to spend a few hours together before rushing home in time for no one to notice we were gone. I visited him at Paula's house, a modest red brick rancher, bursting at the seams with her large black leather furniture and oversized plants. Rakheim's room was a tiny box, almost completely taken up by his bed and a dresser. His bare walls served as a reminder that, as much as Paula tried, he didn't consider this his home.

We went back to having the conversations that made us fall for each other. He told me about his mother, Gina. The way he seemed to soften all over with each new story about her big heart and beautiful smile made me picture her as some sort of angel. Rakheim's father had been murdered and put in the trunk of a car when Rakheim was a boy, so Gina raised him, his brother, and Paula by herself, first in Chicago, where Rakheim was born, and then in Virginia. She married Tina's dad when

Rakheim was in middle school. Because Rakheim was the youngest, she spoiled him with dirt bikes, pagers, and the nicest clothes, but she was a nurse, worked constantly, and their time together was limited. The gifts were deceiving because just keeping a roof over their heads was a struggle for her. The stress caused her to turn to crack, something he suspected Tina's father had introduced her to.

The aneurysm came without warning one afternoon, and she collapsed in pain. Rakheim found her on the floor in the upstairs bathroom, still alive. He wrapped his arms around her while she told him over and over how sorry she was, something, he said, he'd never forget. She lived only a day or two more in the hospital before passing away.

He had no parents, no real home, and dismal grades, but he did have football. Colleges were constantly calling him and sending letters of interest. As a star high-school running back, he had the chance to do something none of his friends and few members of his family could do—go to college. I was excited for him, excited that despite his circumstances, he could earn a degree, but Rakheim didn't share that excitement. College was unfamiliar to him and seemed an unnecessary extension of high school, where, disengaged, he was treated as a dumb athlete by most teachers. Flourishing on the streets, selling, was a clearer, more convenient path with quicker return, more validation, and familiar faces. This is where he focused most of his energy.

Rakheim likely sensed that he was not going to complete college. The American Council on Education would find in their report on race and ethnicity in higher education in 2019, in fact, that Black males working toward their bachelor's degrees were more likely than any other demographic group, including Black females, to drop out after their freshman year. It wasn't enough to just get *into* college on a football scholarship. Rakheim's chances of completing college, as for many Black males, were slim, due to generational poverty, lack of academic preparation, little experience with college in his family, and a more concentrated effort on the "school-to-prison" pipeline than college success by the systems that should have propelled him forward.

Despite these same odds, Joseph, the young father who echoed the weariness I saw in Rakheim and his friends, is now a graduate and an employee of Howard University. In his world, just graduating from high school was an accomplishment. He once told me that growing up, he only knew one person who went to college and earned a degree. His uncle Chris was the sole brother of five on his mother's side who instead of ending up in jail earned a postsecondary credential. This dearth of educational experience and role models combined with scant resources, drug abuse by family members, and teachers and family members calling him "dumb," made college seem an improbable and unattractive proposition for Joseph. "I didn't care about education. I didn't care about college," he explained. It wasn't until he met a few adults at a local youth center who told him he should consider college that he began to think seriously about it, and then they wouldn't take no for an answer.

With little incentive to ask *why* the Black male achievement gap exists, most people would write off Rakheim, Joseph, and most other Black males as simply lazy and unmotivated—a stereotype that can be traced back to the height of the trans-Atlantic slave trade's work to dehumanize Africans and to justify selling their bodies as property. Rakheim didn't need the world to tell him that this devaluation existed, though. You could see that he carried these soul-crushing realities on his shoulders.

After I called to ask him to prom that day, and once he fell in love with me, I became the only positive thing in his life besides football and his family. In the beginning, like everyone else, I didn't really know who Rakheim was, away from the bright lights of the football field, but with each late-night talk, the notoriety, flashy clothes, and money meant less and less. In the quiet moments, when it was just the two of us, he was just Rakheim, open, lighthearted, and playful. I loved him for his warm soul. You considered yourself special for having seen it.

I wish I saw that tender side of Rakheim more. The Rakheim I came to really know was often distant and impenetrable, easily sent into a rage, and prone to taking risks—bigger risks than just speeding on the open highway. This Rakheim was well versed in a foreign, underground language of drugs and guns that I overheard when he was on the phone or standing outside of the car with a friend smoking cigarettes. While I didn't understand the exchanges, I sensed that he was steeped in this world, selling more than just weed. All of this went unsaid but became routine.

When Rakheim was angry, he was eerily unrecognizable. I'd beg him to calm down, but he would be too far away, too consumed with a need to control. I'd scramble to position myself in front of him, thinking if we could just lock eyes—those eyes that always promised safety and security—I could bring him back to me, but he was a stranger beyond my reach. Yelling, shaking, hardly stopping to breath, saying things I never thought he'd say. If he misread a friendly exchange or if I talked about a male friend too often, he called me a "bitch" or a "slut" and would go silent for days. If we argued in the car, he would threaten to throw me out and leave me on the side of the road, or he might drill his finger into my temple to prove a point or shut me up. These scenes were familiar, like angry pencil sketches that furiously danced through my childhood. Now, they were pages in my own sketchbook.

I kept a purple pager in my purse or clipped to my backpack that vibrated when someone was trying to get in contact with me. They could call it, type in their phone number, and then wait for me to call them back. But someone could also put in codes—like "143" for "I love you"—to tell me something without a phone call. If I didn't respond to Rakheim's pages right away, he'd enter the code "187." It came from Section 187 of the California Penal Code, which defined the crime of murder as "the unlawful killing of a human being, or a fetus, with malice aforethought."

I wanted to stop loving Rakheim, but I couldn't. Like so many young women trying to fill needs on the first few levels of Maslow's hierarchy, I felt a sense of security and belonging, even in his anger-filled tirades. And, when they were done, he always apologized with that quiet voice in my ear, telling me it was because he loved me so much that he lost control.

Someone once asked me if I ever felt as if the situations I got myself into with Rakheim were wrong while they were happening. But it was never a matter of right and wrong. I was so determined to get away from the fighting at home that escaping became more important than right and wrong without me even knowing it. To me, my house was the hostile place, not being with Rakheim, not even with his "Tec" around. His prized TEC-9 looked like a small machine gun and held between twenty to fifty rounds. I saw it one day when he ran his hands over it and told me about his lifelong fascination with guns. I should have stopped every-thing then, but as long as *he* was holding it, it couldn't be wrong. I didn't think he'd ever put me in any kind of danger. He promised he'd always protect me. He said he'd do anything for me, even die for me. No one else was willing to do that. And even though I was beginning to see how dangerous Rakheim could be, nothing was worse than the heartbreak of being young and wanting to be loved.

So many of the young women in my program will remind me of my-self at this stage, suffering through dangerous situations just to feel loved and wanted. Young women like Kathy, who came to the US from Bolivia at nine years old and endured years of bullying for not knowing how to speak English. By the time she was a teenager, Kathy was living with extreme depression and had tried to overdose on pills multiple times. She met her son's future father online, after barely graduating from high school, and soon discovered his prescription drug habit and violent be-havior. My heart will ache as she recounts him pushing and choking her while she was pregnant, and when she describes what made it so hard to leave, I instantly understand: "He made me feel so comfortable. It was like nothing mattered except for him. He made me feel like no one else would be there for me except for him."

· · · · ·

Each day, I wrestled with reality and fairy tale, protector and aggressor, reckless chaos and strategic college preparation. At school, with my AP History classmates, I skillfully debated why FDR's Fireside Chats during the Great Depression were so successful. In the afternoons, I gathered in Mrs. Davis's classroom with the rest of the choir to perfect a song before a weekend performance at another church. At home, I sat at the dining room table for hours, meticulously filling out college applications, writing and rewriting my personal essays. Virginia Commonwealth Uni-versity. The College of William & Mary. Hampshire College. Yale Uni-versity. George Washington University. The University of Maryland. When my parents told me they were moving to Washington, DC, after I graduated from high school, being together became more urgent than ever. Each night, Rakheim and I talked on the phone about the various ways we could marry in secret.

Loving Rakheim—and being loved by him—was dark and suffocating, but the brief moments of happiness were brilliant and dazzling enough to keep me captive. They were tiny sparks of make-believe hope and promises that would eventually be broken but helped me get through each day, and I liked the idea of having them—having him—forever, even if it meant losing myself in the process.

CHAPTER 4

TWO PINK LINES

THE TWO PINK LINES formed quickly and clearly. My period was two weeks late, and my breasts were sore. My other attempts to determine if I was pregnant—like trying out Bree's theory that there are more bubbles in your pee when you're expecting—didn't seem reliable, so I went to Kmart and bought a test. Looking through the different types of tests, trying to avoid eye contact with other customers and the cashier, and rushing back to my parents' station wagon in the nearly empty parking lot was an out-of-body experience.

It was three o'clock in the afternoon, right after school. I'd paged Rakheim and told him to meet me at my house. He had swung his Cadillac into my parents' driveway, Nas emanating from the gigantic subwoofers installed in his trunk. It was odd to be there, together, at that time of day. The house was quiet. The bright afternoon sunlight made patterns on the walls and on the furniture in the family room behind us. He stood next to me, smelling familiar. The shampoo he used to wash his dreads that morning was still fragrant, and if I had dug my fingers into his scalp, I would probably have felt his roots were still damp. The smell of Newports, and Black & Milds too, always on his breath and seeped into the fabric of his clothes. He was a mixture of sweet and bitter, endearing and repelling. I held the small white plastic square in my hands, and the two of us watched the pink lines surface, light at first and then darker—like watching magic.

Pregnant.

A hot, fleshy, intense aching. That's what I felt. Like someone had shot me right where the baby was supposed to be. I exhaled slowly, letting my chest sit empty for a moment, almost as a punishment. I needed to feel the physical sting of what had just ripped through my heart. The painful clarity that I was now instantaneously different—inherently bad. Other. I was one of *those girls*, eroding the American family and American society and disappointing everyone who ever cared about me. It happened quickly and without question or hesitation—the transformation from good to bad girl, from right to wrong, from destined for greatness to destined for failure. The moment—even in its swiftness—sent a shock wave through me, defining me wholly and completely.

Without knowing it, I was feeling the impact of a president's words and a country's fears. It was 1998—just three years after President Bill Clinton, in his State of the Union address, called teenage childbearing "our most serious social problem." Not the peak of crime rates in the early 1990s, which had been on the rise since the Lyndon B. Johnson presidency. Not the crack-cocaine epidemic of the mid-1980s. Not the mass incarceration that exploded under President Ronald Reagan, decimating families and disproportionately affecting communities of color. No, young mothers were the greatest threat to our country. Those two pink lines meant that I was now an enemy of the state.

I assumed teen pregnancy was always an epidemic because from the time I was aware of these kinds of things, it was. There was no beginning to it, no emergence. It was understood and accepted as a perpetual plague. I would later learn that, like all things, there *was* a beginning. Teen pregnancy wasn't on the public's radar until the 1950s and 1960s, when teen childbearing reached its highest rates.[1] Then, President Jimmy Carter and nearly every president after him identified it as a priority of their domestic agenda. But it was President Clinton's proclamation that seemed to hurl it into overdrive. It didn't matter that at the time, teen pregnancy rates were drastically lower than twenty-five years earlier—nearly 50 percent lower.

The National Campaign to Prevent Teen and Unplanned Pregnancy was formed just one year after Clinton's State of the Union address. Poll after poll showed that Americans viewed teen pregnancy as a growing problem despite its overall decline. Money was poured into ineffective, fear-based teen pregnancy prevention campaigns that focused on shaming and stigmatizing young women. Few addressed the complexities of teen pregnancy, the issues often in place in a young person's life before a pregnancy, the negative assumptions about people of color that pervade our narrative and thinking on this issue, our own failures in working with families in poverty, or the basic premise that all young people should know they matter regardless of their decisions.

I remember our slender, blonde PE teacher showing some of the ads warning against becoming pregnant on a projector in our sex-ed class along with photos of her own premature baby in an NICU incubator hooked up to tubes. She warned us that teenagers are more likely to have premature babies and asked if we wanted this same fate for our children. I don't remember feeling an overwhelming aversion to sex when I watched her slip a new translucent slide on the humming projector. I do remember, however, feeling that she—like the ads—seemed completely disconnected from me and everyone I knew.

I suppose all of this was weighing on me as we stood so close in that bathroom, with the walls feeling tight around us and the reality of what I held in my hands rushing in all at once. I caught a glimpse of myself in the mirror and wanted to believe that I was watching someone else look at a positive test. A different Nicole. But there I was staring back, with the color drained from my face, both familiar and strangely unfamiliar. I dropped the test on the counter and stumbled back into a ray of sunshine from one of the windows in the family room. I felt its heat on my arm and face, and I could see Rakheim reaching for me through the glaring white.

This could not be happening. I was president of the gospel choir. I was an honor student. I was in AP classes. I had a stack of congratulatory college acceptance letters on my dresser upstairs. I had a plan for my life. I didn't *feel* pregnant. Wouldn't I *feel* something? Why couldn't I *feel* anything?

I finally looked at Rakheim, now sitting across from me on the black couch. He was reclining on a cushion, twisting one of his dreads between his two fingers with an incredulous look on his face. He seemed boyish and awkward in his oversized Avirex jacket, baggy jeans, and untied camel-colored Timberland boots. He was not a father, and I was not a mother.

· · · · ·

"Do you love me, Daddy?"

That was the question my heart asked my father in various ways each day. I would call his attention to my handstand or an original poem I had just scribbled on a napkin in a creative frenzy, trying to distract him from Magic Johnson, Larry Bird, or Andre Tippett dazzling crowds on TV. Other days, when I would wave a stellar report card in his face as he arrived home from work or announce a distinction I had received at school over dinner, the question was, "Are you proud of me?" I never *really* asked him either of those questions, and I never called him "Daddy." "Daddy" was for little girls who had their fathers wrapped around their fingers. I imagined that those fathers and daughters went fishing together and sat on their porches talking for hours. They argued about boyfriends because those kinds of fathers were annoyingly overprotective. That wasn't us. We didn't fish, or spend hours together, or talk about those kinds of things. He didn't even ask me about my friends or boyfriends. If we had talked about those things, it would have been one of the relationships that would have most influenced my decisions about relationships and sex.

My father had a contemplative look about him that made you aware of his presence in a room or even somewhere in the house. He was reflective, pensive, always with two fingers pressed to his chin and that arm resting on the other, folded across his stomach. When he wasn't smiling, his face was like rich, brown clay chiseled into thought. This is how you found him after a long commute home as a corporate film producer in Boston and then later as a college administrator. Late into the night, he stood like that, holding his rum and Coke, listening to his jazz, the floor vibrating to the rhythm of the unpredictable genius of John Coltrane, Miles Davis, or Hugh Masekela. They provided the background music of my childhood. At times romantic and whimsical. At times angry and jarring. Musicians were the only people who seemed to make my father truly happy. He mimicked their fingers dancing up and down the keys of an imaginary trumpet or saxophone or piano, calling for us to watch and listen and then laughing to himself when we couldn't truly appreciate their music the way he did.

Jazz played while he told his stories about the civil rights movement and its heroes or his Peace Corps days in Nigeria in the late 1960s helping to plant crops and teach children. It played when he told us where he was when Martin Luther King Jr. was shot and how his college roommates at Tennessee State asked him to join them for a sit-in with the future congressman John Lewis. I curled up in the big maple chair with the soft orange cushions, which traveled from city to city with us each time he got a new job. I heard those stories over and over until I could tell them myself. They shaped and molded me. Like my dad, I found myself enthralled by the work of *change*, feeling the tiny spark of possibility that I, too, had a voice that could be useful someday.

I learned over time that if I wanted my father to *see* me, if I wanted his full attention, my handstands and poems would not do the trick. A question about Nigeria or Jesse Jackson or an idea I had for a service project at school were the inquiries that would pull him away from his jazz or from where he sat for hours at the dining room table, his fingers dancing around the keys of his prized typewriter in the same way they danced up and down his imaginary instruments.

As I got older, though, I was less interested in devising plans to get his attention. I didn't want to hear his stories or jazz music anymore. My heart kept asking the same questions, but it no longer hung in the balance, waiting for the answers.

. . . . .

The silence pulled a deceptive cloak of normalcy over everything. The calm almost made you believe the world was not upside down. Rakheim still sat there on the couch, quiet, and I was still slumped in the chair. It was maddening.

I ran upstairs, threw myself on my bed, and let out waves of grief into my pillow. I cried so hard, it was difficult to breathe, and for a moment,

I wondered if this would hurt the baby. My world—everything I'd built, everything my parents were expecting of me—was gone.

I felt Rakheim beside me with his hand on my back. It was the same hand that used to caress my skin, play with my hair, and wipe my tears, but now it was heavy and strange.

"Shhhh, baby. We're gonna be alright." And then I heard the happiness in his voice. "We're gonna have a baby. Is that bad?"

I looked up at him, pushing the curls from my face and sniffling back my tears. For the first time, I watched him climb down from the pedestal I'd put him on. Yes, he was impulsive, short-tempered, and combative, but to me, he always knew what was best. He had lived a harder life and had accumulated a wisdom in his short eighteen years that I could only pretend to understand. Now, his words peeled all of that back to reveal someone even lonelier and more unsure than I was.

There was also something that I couldn't articulate then, but something I inherently knew. It was that, as Black teens, Rakheim and I lived each day with an intangible uncertainty—a nagging and constant questioning of any optimism for the future. Tiger Woods had just won the Masters Tournament in Augusta, Georgia, becoming the first African-American and youngest golfer to win the title. But we were also still reeling from the acquittal of the three police officers tried in the horrific beating of a Black man, Rodney King, and the resulting three-day riot in Los Angeles that left more than fifty people dead and immeasurable devastation. If one moment swept us into a sense of assurance, the next moment reminded us of who we were and our place in the world.

One of those moments happened when I was twelve during a trip down to Daytona Beach to visit my dad's family and Disney World. My first time at the theme park was all I could think about as our rental car traveled along a major roadway in the haze of the humid August evening. Disney World was a luxury for our family. We couldn't afford multiple days at the park or a stay at a fancy Disney resort. Instead, we settled in at a cheap hotel far away from Disney and would rely on my cousin, Buzzy, who worked for Disney World, to get us all in for free. I understood how special and rare this was. I was excited. The feeling that something magical was going to happen the next day also settled me and centered me as we cruised along. Yes, tomorrow would be amazing.

And then the moment shifted, slipping into something precarious and fragile. The conversation between my mom and dad that had been a bubbling back-and-forth banter about the family BBQ earlier that day halted abruptly in the front seat. A thick hush fell over the car, which by now had slowed down to a complete stop in the dirt on the side of the road. I swung my head around to see red and blue lights flashing against a rich pink and orange sky behind us. A White man in uniform stepped out with a stern face and black sunglasses. He slowly walked up to the driver's side of the car and leaned down toward the open window where my dad sat stiffly. He peered in, his eyes scanning the three of us.

"You have an ID?" he asked my father, in a tone that was more appropriate for speaking to a boy rather than a grown man.

Cutting the silence in the car, my father responded in a voice so deferential and strange that I almost didn't recognize it. It was soft, slow, and deliberate, almost as if he was trying to convince this officer of something important without actually saying the words.

"Yes, sir." He never looked at the officer. He kept his gaze low as he slowly reached for his wallet.

My eyes, blurring with tears, drilled into the back of my father's head, searching for something that would help me understand what was happening and who this new version of my father was. But it took only a few seconds for my brain to refer back to our many talks about the dangers of the South. It pulled up the photographs he had shown me of Emmett Till's mutilated face as he lay in a casket after a deadly visit to Mississippi and the haunting, lifeless bodies of Blacks across the South hanging from large oak trees. I remembered this danger had no geographical boundaries, playing back in my head the news reports of Rodney King's LAPD beating just one year earlier. And it cautioned me that these were not just historical events in books and documentaries. These were present and future realities.

Five years later, in 1998, the year that Rakheim and I would be preparing to walk across the graduation stage, three White men would kidnap a Black man, James Byrd, in Texas, beat him, slit his throat, chain him by the ankles to the back of a pickup truck then drag him for three and a half miles down a country road. Byrd would die after being decapitated. This evil would shock the nation. Of course, at the time I sat in the back seat of that car with the police lights flashing around us that night in Florida, Byrd was alive, but the scenario of what would happen to him and what *could* happen to my father in that moment was plausible and crushing.

My father's brain had played all of this through long before mine because it had to. Because if you don't think ahead, you leave yourself and your family vulnerable. From a childhood spent in the South, he intrinsically knew what sociologists at the University of Michigan, Rutgers University, and Washington University would discover more than two decades later: about one in one thousand Black men and boys will die at the hands of police officers over the course of their lives.

He was now laser-focused. He knew that he was a Black man in a car with a White woman and a biracial child at night in the South, and we were not safe. To protect us, he had to be unthreatening and communicate, without words, that he understood his place, which had to be much lower than this White police officer. And this role that he had to play, so completely different from the strong presence of a father that I knew, just to safeguard us, broke my heart. It made our visit less sweet, Disney World less magical, my father less chiseled, the future less bright, and the world more treacherous.

I never forgot this moment, and later in life, I would take it—along with all of the others that followed—into my work with young people. It taught me that, particularly for Black and Brown youth, institutions we often think of as dependable and trustworthy, like schools, the police force, social services, even community programs, can be unreliable or unpredictable, requiring young people to watch their footing, always expecting a sinkhole where there should be solid ground. This uncertainty can impact their decisions, views of the world, and thoughts about their future in ways that are often hard for others to make sense of. My youth work would lean into this brutal reality, embrace it, and serve young people with a relentless consistency that they might not find anywhere else.

By the time we were seniors in high school, these kinds of moments had piled one on top of the other for Rakheim and me. We found ourselves at such a pivotal time—the end of something and the beginning of something else. We were about to embark on the rest of our lives. The world should have been at our feet, but we were acutely aware of the *potential* for progress and success but never the promise or guarantee. For Rakheim, an orphaned football prodigy, this baby—as unexpected and untimely as it might be—represented one of the rare assurances in his life. A happiness he could truly hold on to. A permanence that no one could take away from him.

"Is it so bad? Yes. Yes, it's bad, Rakheim. I have to go to college! I can't be a mom!"

"You can do all that, boo. I'm gonna take care of you." He smoothed my curls back and rested his hand on my head. "I always wanted you to have my baby."

I felt sick. Maybe because of the baby and maybe because of him. I motioned toward the alarm clock by my bed. "You should go. My mom might come home early from work."

· · · · ·

If my father's jazz provided the soundtrack of my childhood, my mother's artwork was the backdrop. Her paintings, large and small, watercolors and oils, filled the guest rooms and basements of all of the houses we lived in. Sometimes, they would take over the kitchens too because she preferred the large windows and sunlight they offered to perfect a detail in her work. She would cut pages of artwork from the large books that lined our bookshelves and pin them to a corkboard or tape them on the walls. Degas. Frida Kahlo. Georgia O'Keeffe. Gauguin. Robert Colescott. Alma Thomas. As a little girl, I would work alongside my mother for hours because I wanted to share this world with her. I understood that art, for her, was both a compulsion and an escape. When she was painting or drawing, she was consumed and happy, but she was never so absorbed that she couldn't stop and talk to me or let me pull up a stool beside her. In this world, there was always room for both of us.

Her parents recognized and encouraged her talent early on, regularly driving her into downtown New Haven, about fifteen minutes from their two-story brick house in a middle-class Connecticut neighborhood, for art lessons. They bought her pencils and drawing pads, and they proudly displayed her paintings around the house. When she applied to college, my grandfather was teaching chemical engineering at Yale University. He and my grandmother, who was a homemaker, lived a deliberately modest life in order to save enough money for her and my mother's younger brother and sister to go to school without racking up debt.

We come to college to be educated. My mother went to Boston University with this expectation. She received an education not just in the arts but in the masterful ways that we mask our ugly realities—our secrets. Boston in the 1960s was still attempting to bask in its abolitionist history while at the same time battling segregated schools, the consequences of urban renewal, housing discrimination, and more. While the South outwardly wrestled with its racist history, the North painted a pretty picture of "accidental" segregation, obscuring deliberate policies and legislation that created long-standing walls between Blacks and Whites. Even my mother—a bright-eyed, naive girl from a small New England town who had attended an all-White Catholic girls' school—could see that the paint was peeling.

In Boston, she honed her craft, studying artists who grappled with human tragedy. She knew, in this new place with these new, exciting people, that she wanted to live life differently, freely, and unapologetically. She wanted to challenge the unintended or overt ways that the world tried to separate and oppress people. And when she met and married my father, whose own vision for challenging the status quo she found mesmerizing, she was pursuing that freedom and showing the world yet another new, beautiful creation—a family formed from two different worlds.

When I see pictures of my mother during this time, in the early 1970s, before she became a mother, she has long hair parted in the middle, creamy skin, and perfect rose-colored lips. She is lovely, eager, and optimistic. In her vibrant smile, I can tell that she believes a paintbrush can change the world—can make it right. She is an artist. She has spent her entire life learning how to make things pleasing. She believes she can fix anything.

When I come along just a few years later, I will love this about her. I will love her brightness and attempts to keep any ugliness, whether in our house or out in the world, at bay. I will gravitate to her when I'm angry or defeated because she will stop everything—even a painting—to put a smile on my face. I will, without knowing it, conjure her same optimism when I find out that I am pregnant at seventeen, and I will model my own mothering after hers because I will know how good it feels to be on the receiving end of that love. There will come a time, years later, when she realizes that she can't fix everything and that her powers can only go so far, but by then, it's too late. The seeds of hopefulness have already been planted and have taken root inside of me, and forever and always, I will be a believer.

I came into young motherhood with many advantages, a significant one being that I had a loving, caring mother. So many of the students I will meet years later will have to navigate parenting without the benefit of a role model and without being raised with the nurturing that we all need and deserve. During one of my sessions with an incoming class of freshmen, a young woman in the back with a large Afro puff ponytail and a bright smile will raise her hand. She'll ask me if it's possible for the organization to start providing more parenting skills and support. Her explanation for this question will break my heart: "My mother is strung out on drugs, and my dad is incarcerated. When I was in labor, my mom couldn't even help me. I didn't know what was happening to my body. I don't have anyone who can model parenting for me, and I want to be a good mom." A few months later, we will launch our early-childhood program, which will provide monthly home visits focused on helping our "Scholars," as we will come to call them, become their children's first teachers.

· · · · ·

I watched my mom while we sat at the dining room table looking over my college acceptance letters. She was soft. Her arms were smooth to the touch with just a slight layer of blonde peach fuzz that made you want to curl up and go to sleep in them. She had no idea what was happening inside me each day. The guilt I felt when I was around her outweighed any anxieties I had about the baby. I was sure she would collapse or crumble, and then of course, she would put herself back together again, but like a tea cup that has been nicked, there would always be a crack or two right along the surface. And I would always see those cracks and know that I was the cause.

My heart ached for her. Now that I was growing this little person, I tried to picture what it was going to look like and what it would grow up to be. I was beginning to feel a parent's love for their child, wanting to give them the world before you have even given them their first bottle. I wished I could go back in time to change everything just for *her*, but in the days after the two pink lines, I understood that you can never go back. You are the person your past delivers to you, and the person your future calls for.

"Would you love me no matter what I did?" I asked her one day as we made dinner together in the kitchen. I steadied an onion on the cutting board with one hand and held a knife in the other. I had been pretending to listen to whatever we were talking about for a while now, but my mind was consumed with the secret and how it would change everything. She had been fluttering around me, adding spices to the pot of bubbling tomato sauce.

She stopped and turned to look at me. She was so much shorter than me now. Her slender cream-colored arm wrapped around my waist, and she laughed nervously.

"Of course."

I didn't tell anyone. In my mind, I had to have all of the answers first. I needed a plan. My first job as a cashier at Kmart the year before was just for spending money to go to the movies or buy myself a shirt at the mall. I had quit after just a few months so I could concentrate on AP Statistics. Now, I needed money for what was coming, for grown-up things. I immediately got a job as an operator for an alphanumeric-paging company. It involved me sitting in a call center for hours taking messages for doctors and then sending those messages to a pager on their hip as they walked through hospital halls. It was miserable. The pay wasn't good. The supervisors weren't understanding. I wasn't there long, and I'd already gotten demerits for morning sickness in the bathroom and not knowing where to report on my first day. I had always been a hard worker, but what kind of jobs were available to me without a high school diploma or college degree? The reality of my situation was setting in. If I stopped here, if I didn't go to college, I would be like most of the teen moms I knew. I would have no option but to work in retail or some type of service job, which meant little pay, few benefits, difficult schedules, and only a small window in the whirlwind of my shift work to actually see my child.

My child. It was hard to wrap my mind around this, but the idea that I was now more than just me was slowly starting to sink in. One night I sat on the floor of my room and pulled my shirt up over my belly button. I looked down at my flat stomach, and for the first time, I laid my hand across it.

I sort of floated through the halls at school—there but not really. I was completely distracted by what was happening inside of me both physically and emotionally. None of my teachers noticed their honor roll student's sudden fatigued look or lack of normal excitement and interest in what we were studying. None of them asked me to stay after class so they could see what was wrong. It was business as usual, expecting me to show up, expecting me to turn in my work, never expecting a pregnancy.

But a secret like this can be too much to carry alone. I needed to tell someone, and one day, in the cafeteria during lunch, I told Bree while the world seemed to spin backwards around us. She slapped her hands down on the table, eyes wide. Then she started digging through her purse, to find a pen.

"I'm going to give you the name of the place I went to. It was a while ago, but I bet it's still there. Was it in Norfolk? I think it was."

She was talking about the clinic she went to for her abortion in the seventh grade.

"I'm not getting rid of it," I said, looking down as I swirled my frosted flakes around in my bowl with my finger. The flakes were too soggy and now made my stomach turn.

"You're *keeping* it?"

I was crazy. How was I going to take care of a baby? Rakheim didn't even have a job. We didn't even live together. More than likely, we wouldn't even stay together. Did I want to raise a baby on my own? How was I going to go to college? People just don't bring babies to college. I was just going to throw everything away? My future?

My pregnancy and my decision to keep the baby cast me out on an island, and the distance between me and everyone else grew greater by the day. I was different now. Not only because of my pregnancy but also because I wasn't terminating it. Despite the fact that several of my friends had had abortions, including Bree—nearly 25 percent of all teen pregnancies end with an abortion[2]—I couldn't see myself terminating the pregnancy. Maybe it was my Catholic upbringing. Maybe it was how much I loved kids. Maybe it was because I had always imagined that, one day, I'd be a mother. Getting to know other young mothers years later, I'll hear different stories about why they didn't get abortions. Some simply couldn't afford it, some discovered their pregnancies too late to terminate, and others felt pressured by their partner or family to keep the baby.

There were no easy decisions, no easy answers, only an impossible path forward. I didn't blame Bree or others later for being frustrated with me. I was frustrated with me too. But I couldn't be concerned with friendships anymore. All I could do was exist. That's all I could manage.

The news about my pregnancy spread quickly beyond Bree, to people I didn't even know. The rumors started soon after. I had purposefully gotten pregnant to trap Rakheim so he wouldn't leave me before he went off to play college football at some Division I school. I wasn't even pregnant. I was lying just to get attention. No one asked me how I was feeling. No one told me that right now things were difficult, but everything would be fine. No one said that I didn't have to put my dreams on hold. People just avoided me.

When young women discover their pregnancies, and after they have their babies, many find themselves on this same dark and isolated island. I was experiencing firsthand the way we treat teen mothers—the shaming, the avoidance, and the dismal predictions we make about their futures—and how this treatment contributes to their higher rates of depression.[3] We talk about postpartum depression, but we only talk about it for *some* mothers. We don't talk about it for teen mothers, even though they are experiencing postpartum depression and related postpartum mood disorders at nearly double the rate of all mothers. And we don't talk about the role we play in heightening these numbers at a time when they need our love and encouragement the most.

Through Chelsea's story, years later, I will come to understand how drastic the effects of this can be. She will tell me that after she was disowned by her family because of her pregnancy, she slipped into a deep depression. At first, she hated her unborn daughter. With a shaking voice, she will admit to even hitting her stomach to end the pregnancy. She will struggle to forgive herself for this: "Even today, I beat myself up about it. She didn't ask to be here." When her growing belly became too obvious to hide, her teachers found ways to remove her from their classrooms, mostly by placing her in in-school suspension. She didn't begin to feel differently about the baby until, one day, "I woke up, and I was looking at ultrasound pictures and I had heard her heartbeat, and it was like everything changed in that moment. I decided I didn't want her life to be like mine."

.....

I sat in AP English one day and looked around at all the other students. They were laughing and joking, talking about the senior prom. Right now, I was thinking about adult things. Finding an ob-gyn. Getting a better-paying job. Trying to reconcile a baby and a college degree. I buried my head in my folded arms on my desk to hide my face. The teacher walked over and asked if I was okay. I shook my head. She wrote me a pass to go see my guidance counselor. Instead I went to Mrs. Walker's room.

Mrs. Walker was a teacher in the school's gifted program.

I wasn't extremely close to Mrs. Walker, and that's probably why she was the first adult I told about my pregnancy. She was safe. If she judged me harshly, it wouldn't hurt as much. But she didn't judge me. She held me. And that's what I remember most about that day in her room—how good it felt to cry with someone. Her arms wrapped around me, and she told me it was going to be okay. She didn't show any surprise or disappointment. Just a sadness. And then, after a while, she lifted my chin so our eyes met, and she wiped my tears.

"You should call your mom right now." She placed a hand on the black phone on her desk. "She loves you, Nicole. This isn't going to change that, sweetie, I promise."

After she wrote down the name and phone number of her gynecologist, she left me alone in the room. I held the phone in my hand. I hung it back up. This was a mistake. But then the desire to not be so alone overtook me, and I dialed my mom's number at work.

"Mom?"

"Nicole, what's wrong? Are you pregnant?"

"Yes."

Then she said, "We'll talk later. We'll have to talk when I get home."

I left Mrs. Walker's room. The hallways, the lockers, everything seemed so small now. I'd met friends, stressed about tests and gotten into arguments in those hallways. I'd walked hand in hand with a couple of boyfriends and laughed and joked in those hallways. That's where I'd gotten to know Rakheim. I could hear the echo of all of those things now. Graduation was months away, but I felt like I had already moved on from all of this.

· · · · ·

I heard the front door close and my mother put down her bags and move around in the kitchen. I imagined her face, heavy with disappointment. Upstairs, I sat on my bed, my hands tightly gripped together on my lap, waiting. She'd already been crying during the forty-five-minute drive home from Newport News, where she was teaching. When she appeared at my door, she looked older and tired. Her mascara turned to black smudges around her glassy eyes.

She sat next to me on the bed and let out a deep, shaky breath. "I can't believe this is happening."

I reached my arms around her and rested my head on her shoulder. Tears skated down my cheeks. I didn't wipe them. I let them fall on my arm.

"Now you won't be able to go to college, Nicole. Do you know that?" She spoke slowly and carefully so I would understand how bad the situation was. "What are you going to do?"

She knew what I was too young to know: most girls who get pregnant don't graduate from college before they turn thirty—in fact, barely 2 percent.[4] She knew that less than half even graduate from high school, and they—along with their children—are likely to live in poverty, struggling to put food on the table and keep a roof over their heads. She knew that a friend at her Catholic girls' school who had gotten pregnant disappeared and was never heard from again. It was during a time when women were just beginning to challenge the confines of traditional roles and pursue their education and careers. The answer to a teen pregnancy was still to send a young girl away, make her disappear, force her to give up her baby, and then return to life as if nothing ever happened.

"I'm going to go to college." I tried to say it with strength and assurance, but I wasn't so sure of it myself. I knew I wanted it, but I didn't know if I was *crazy* to want it. I didn't actually know if it was possible.

None of the girls I knew at Tallwood who got pregnant went on to college. Most continued working at whatever retail jobs they'd picked up in high school—even Alexis, an older girl I befriended when we were both in an after-school club that encouraged minority students to pursue careers in science, technology, engineering, and mathematics. While I did well in math, I had to work hard at it, but Alexis was bored by even the most difficult equations. She was taking AP Calculus, and sailing through. She was so bright and seemed to make all the right decisions. I was just as baffled by the fact that she was pregnant as I was by my AP Stats homework.

This was on my mind as we boarded a yellow school bus to visit the Virginia Air and Space Center, and Alexis wobbled down the aisle toward a seat. By the time she settled in by the window, she let her forehead fall on the glass and took two deep breaths while she rubbed her large belly. I asked if I could touch it, and she smiled wide, grabbed my hand and placed it on her stomach. I remember being surprised by how hard it was. During the ride, I stumbled, without thinking, into a question about which college she was going to, and that was the only time I ever saw her smile fade. She gazed out the window as neighborhoods and trees flashed by then said, "I can't do any of that now." A few weeks after the field trip, she stopped coming to school. People said she had her baby and decided not to come back, but sometimes she was spotted at the Wendy's around the corner from Tallwood—where she worked.

"No, you won't, Nicole. You don't know. You have no idea," my mom said, putting her palm against her forehead and then running her fingers through her hair, making it messy and disheveled. "It's going to be so hard."

"Watch, Mom. I promise you, I'll be in college in one year. In 1999, I'll start school. I'm just going to take a year off, to, you know, have the baby. No matter what, I'm going to college."

We stayed like that for a while, just the two of us alone in the house, no urgency to untangle ourselves and get dinner started. Anika was away at Yale. My dad was in Washington, DC. It was just me and my mother on that spring Virginia evening, anchored there by my secret and the choice of either letting it tear us apart or deliver us into the next day.

CHAPTER 5

INTO THE DARK

A STUFFED BLACK PLASTIC TRASH BAG. That was the sum of who I was and a mishmash of necessities for the new life ahead. I dragged it across the lawn by the thin red strings that cinched it tightly shut to where Rakheim's Cadillac sat, parked in front of my parents' house. He hurled it into the trunk next to the other one I'd brought out to him a few minutes before.

"That's it?" he asked.

"Yep," I said even though that *wasn't* it.

There was so much more in my room upstairs. Stuffed animals, journals, tapes and CDs, pictures, my pet turtle, Peppermint. These were things that, a few weeks ago, before the baby, I wouldn't have been able to live without. Now, it felt like a part of me was getting in the car with Rakheim while the rest of me stood in my bedroom window watching incredulously. I'd been planning to leave for a long time but not like this. I envisioned a months-long process guided by a thorough checklist from my university, shopping trips to Kmart for washcloths and shower bins, and weeks of methodical packing and designing my soon-to-be dorm room. This was instead premature—a too-soon severing of my childhood. Abrupt. But I couldn't say that to Rakheim, someone whose life had been upended without warning time after time and who had learned to live without more important things—he had lost people, parents, and homes. And I couldn't let my mom and dad, who stood on the doorstep watching us pack the bags into Rakheim's car, see that I was having second thoughts about leaving.

We walked around to the front of the car, opened the doors, and got inside. As Rakheim turned the key, his speakers belted out whatever rap song he'd been listening to when he arrived a few minutes before. I squinted at my parents in the afternoon sun. They waved, seemingly indifferent as we slowly pulled off. Later, my mom would admit they expected I'd be back in a few days.

• • • • •

Mothers share childbirth stories. We marvel at how varied and universal the experience of bringing life into the world can be. How did you know you were in labor? When did your water break? How long did you have to push? Did you get a C-section? Each time we share, there is a healing for traumas and an immediate connection in our collective experience. Those of us who were young mothers also share "reaction stories." How did your family react when you told them you were pregnant? What did they do? What did *you* do? Each story brings us back to our own moment of truth—when we stood on that same cliff, our feet clinging to the edge of normalcy while slipping into the dark.

Nija, a student in my program and an aspiring orthodontist, will tell me her reaction story years later, and it will also involve the things she cherished most and a front yard. At thirteen, after a rocky childhood with a mother whose mental health issues were exacerbated by a house fire in which they lost everything, she lobbied to move in with her father. His house would present an escape from her mother's suffocating illness and a world of new opportunities. While she excelled academically, in high school, she was consumed with overcoming a learning disability, shouldering the separation from her mother and sister, and trying to live up to her dad's expectations. When her father found out she was pregnant, in a rage, he scattered the contents of her room—her clothes, mementos, and other belongings—on the grass in front of their Cleveland home. She'd kept it from her father because she was afraid he would become violent as he had been in the past. It was her seventeenth birthday.

Another student, Ana, who became pregnant at sixteen, will tell me a different reaction story. Consumed with worry about how her religious

Salvadoran family would take the news, she hid her entire pregnancy. Her mother was raising five children in a one-bedroom apartment. She was like a blur, working multiple jobs in restaurants and cleaning buildings, dropping the kids off with different friends on the weekends and asking the school secretaries or counselors to take them after school during the week. "I don't remember her ever going to a parent-teacher conference," she will tell me. By the time Ana is in high school, she is hungry for someone to see her—to take an interest in her. She meets the father of her child—someone who will abandon her when she tells him she is pregnant and will never meet his son. Her pregnancy will be lonely with no one to talk to about what is happening to her body and only one visit to the doctor right before she gives birth. "We had nothing," she tells me, "no car seat or crib." Her family will find out only two weeks before her son is born, leaving little time for judgment or support. "The mother part, I didn't know what to do. As much as my mom wanted to help, she had to go to work."

Others—young and old—will tell me they were kicked out of their parents' houses, forced to leave their schools, and made to stand up in church to repent for their sins. I will only hear a few stories of families working through their pain and devastation to ensure their son or daughter was able to continue their education, but those are the stories I will yearn for.

My reaction story was a prolonged blow to my support system, beginning with my mother that day, but dragging on with my dad and Anika. While my mom was at first too overwhelmed with grief for all I was losing and for how difficult things would be, she soon opened herself up to what I was trying to carve out from the carnage—a way forward. The house was quiet, with few conversations between us, but when she did force an exchange over dinner, and the topic of college came up, she listened to my plans, trying hard to lift her smile into a hopeful and agreeable expression. This was a test of all of the optimism she had, and she was struggling to hang on to it.

Anika was less open to my way forward. At first, she bubbled over, telling my mom it was my parents' fault for not talking to me about sex and for all of the arguing that went on in our house. The fact that in the midst of finding out I was pregnant, they didn't do anything to celebrate my eighteenth birthday—no cake, no card—pushed her over the edge. It felt good to have someone on my side, someone who advocated for me, but that feeling was short-lived.

Anika's support was contingent on me giving up the baby and moving on with my life. I could go off to college as planned, and the pregnancy would just be a blip in the radar—a faded, bad dream that would eventually disappear. I told her I didn't want an abortion. She then mailed me a packet of information on adoption. The day she called from her apartment in Connecticut to ask if I received it, I mustered the courage to tell her I couldn't give up the baby either. I already felt something for it, I explained, and I had to find a way to take care of it, even if that meant a totally different life than the one I'd always envisioned. This was hard for her, someone who relied on solid, practical plans, perfect calculations, and invariable straight lines. She insisted that I stay in Virginia Beach with my parents if I wanted to keep the baby. I told her Rakheim and I were planning to move in together. She told me my head was in the "fucking" clouds, and she never wanted to talk to me again. After she slammed down the phone, the dial tone reminded me of how completely alone I was.

The day after I told my mom, she called me into her bedroom and handed me the phone. I sat on the side of their bed, near the nightstand, and put the phone to my ear. My dad's flat, matter-of-fact voice asked if it was true that I was pregnant. Softly, I said yes, and he told me to give the phone back to my mother. That was the extent of our conversation about my pregnancy. I didn't expect much emotion except anger, but that would come later, and it wouldn't be the pregnancy that would light the fuse; it would be a bad grade.

I'd gotten a D in one of my classes—ironically, in journalism. Even though my teachers had been informed of my pregnancy so they might be more sympathetic to what I was experiencing both physically and emotionally, my journalism teacher resented the idea of any special treatment. She refused to let me catch up on late assignments, graded my papers more harshly, and wouldn't look me in the eye when I tried to talk to her about my work. My favorite class soon became my most dreaded, and my grade slipped from an A to that D.

My dad was back from Washington, DC, when my report card—a piece of paper that once meant so much to me—arrived. It used to be the thing that validated me and endeared me to him, but now, with a baby growing inside me and a future to figure out, that's all it really was—a piece of paper. To my dad, though, it was still everything. He could leave the pregnancy to my mother, but academics were still his territory, and he wasn't willing to make concessions for the whirlwind that was happening inside of me and in our home. A bad grade was grounds for punishing me without ever having to say a word about the baby.

That day, he was in my face, yelling, our noses almost touching, and he gripped the crumpled report card—the evidence—in his hand. With his temper at its peak, I wanted to melt into the wall behind me. He had that look that used to make my insides shake when I was a little girl. Now, just a few days after my eighteenth birthday, my insides were shaking.

We argued. He took my car keys and told me I'd have to find my own way to the doctor. I told him I was leaving, and I called Rakheim to come get me. When I made that call and that proclamation, I hadn't given much thought to where we would go. We always talked about leaving everything and everyone and running off together, but we never discussed the details. Now, I was too consumed with this moment and all of its pain to ask the right questions and to determine if I was about to go from one tumultuous situation into another. This argument with my dad wasn't unrivaled in its severity. In fact, the chaos was familiar. It was the baby that made everything different. I felt the need to protect the tiny life inside of me from the heartache and anxiety I had learned to cope and coexist with. I was pushed to leave not because my dad had never been that angry but because I now had something that needed shielding and safeguarding.

I enjoyed the freedom of not having a curfew or anyone to answer to for only that first day. Rakheim and I drove around in the warmth of the evening with my trash bags in the trunk while I reflected on what the past few weeks had done to my life, and he called around trying to find a place for us to stay. Paula agreed to let us come to her house, but she made it clear that it could only be temporary. We settled into his tiny room after his cousins had gone to bed, but the next day, when the sun rose, reality crept in. Life without my family was difficult and empty. I had to make each day worthwhile without them, and then soon without Rakheim.

At the time, I had no idea how common my displacement was or that homelessness and teen pregnancy were so intertwined. A study conducted in 2013 by the Massachusetts Alliance on Teen Pregnancy will find that 30 percent of the state's teen parents will be homeless at some point. In New York City, in 2017, young parents and their children will account for more than 70 percent of the city's homeless youth.[1] That same year, in DC, where my organization's office will be located, nearly half of the seven hundred families in the city's largest homeless shelter will be headed by someone younger than twenty-four,[2] usually a Black or Brown single mom. Through my work, I'll learn that some young parents become pregnant *while* homeless, some become homeless as a *direct consequence* of their pregnancy, and others struggle to keep a roof over their heads while *trying to provide* for their family. Underlying each of these situations will be a string of failed interventions from systems that should have been providing nurturing, safety, and support, and our programming will have to compensate for these failures.

After a few nights at Paula's, we moved in with a lesbian couple renting a townhouse off Lynnhaven Parkway about twenty minutes away.

Rakheim and I stayed in an extra room off of the kitchen that was overcrowded, with a king-sized bed and large TV. If you came in the room, there wasn't much to do except sit or lie on the bed. I spent most of my time in the room alone. After a few days in that house, I felt displaced, isolated, not sure where home was. The move quickly propelled me into a much harder life than I'd known—a foreign and lonely existence that would challenge my notions about poverty and the "right" decisions.

When we moved in with Yvonne and Sharon, I had two months left in my senior year. The daily dilemma was trying to find a way to get to Tallwood each morning. When Rakheim's Cadillac was working, I'd drop him off at Norcom in Portsmouth and then head back to Virginia Beach for my first class at 9 a.m. But when the car broke down, we were forced to rely on friends to get us to school, and they didn't always come through. Occasionally, Yvonne would drop us off, but the longer I stayed, the more she resented me, so that was rare. The tardies and absences began to stack up, and like many pregnant girls, my attendance became an issue. In what seemed like an overnight transformation, I was now one of *those* students who wasn't showing up for school—the ones I used to look at disapprovingly. I now desperately needed teachers and administrators to see past my pregnancy and ask *why* my seat was constantly empty—something that doesn't happen enough.

School became strange and uncertain. My time there felt scarce and stolen and lost in a whole day of difficult choices. I came to understand the real reason why Alexis, my mom's high school friend, and so many other girls just disappeared. It wasn't a shift in our priorities, with school being less important than working or some relationship. It was a consequence of our unstable situations and losing what little control we had. Years later, when I discover the statistic that less than 50 percent of teen mothers even graduate from high school, it will bring me back to this point when I walked Tallwood's halls like a ghost, and graduation seemed impossible. It will remind me of the havoc a teen pregnancy can instantly inflict on even the most promising young person's life.

It seemed like each crisis fed the next. I quit my job at the paging company because I couldn't keep up with the strict schedule, especially without reliable transportation. I didn't have a weekly ten-dollar allowance anymore, and Rakheim had never worked a real job so there was no steady income. This created an instant tension between us and Yvonne because we were supposed to be paying rent, but most of the time, she and Sharon would just ask Rakheim to come up to their room and compensate them by giving them some of his weed. Yvonne expected me to pull my weight like everyone else, but Rakheim told her I needed to concentrate on graduating and staying healthy. He was selling constantly now—whenever he wasn't at school—but despite his many hours on the streets, we never had enough money. We were caught in what seemed like a never-ending cycle.

"We can use that to get a place, and then you won't have to sell anymore," I'd say excitedly, sitting on the bed watching him count hundreds of dollars in piles of twenties, tens, fives, and ones in the middle of the night.

"Nah, baby," he'd say, kissing me on my forehead. "We need this to re-up."

But using the money to buy more drugs never resulted in more money. I couldn't help but feel like he, Yvonne, and Sharon were smoking away the little money we could have had. And I hated the fact that he was even selling at all—that he was a cog in the wheels of a deep operation sucking the life from addicts, Black men who were necessary for it to thrive, and communities that were ravaged by it. Each night, I worried he wouldn't come home because he was in either a hospital or a jail. This daily fear for the father of my unborn baby was valid—even though Blacks and Whites sell drugs at the same rate, Rakheim was 2.7 times more likely to be arrested for drug-related offenses.[3] I convinced myself that soon he'd be in college, playing football, and he wouldn't have to sell anymore. This was all temporary.

We ate fast food and occasionally home-cooked meals at Paula's house. Sometimes Yvonne made dinner, but the food was so bad it was hard to stomach no matter how hungry we were. I quickly gained an appreciation for all of the things my parents used to provide. Three meals a day. Deodorant. Lotion. Shampoo. Sometimes I had to go without these things and make do with whatever I could find in the kitchen and bathroom cabinets, which was never much. I had to be creative. Having no money and no transportation forced me to develop survival skills that were never necessary before.

I didn't feel clean. I didn't feel beautiful. I struggled every morning to make myself presentable for school. My two trash bags barely contained enough for pajamas and a week's worth of basic outfits. The only pretty things I had were the gold hoop earrings I'd worn the day I left my parents' house. I put them on every morning hoping they'd divert attention away from the rest of me. I didn't recognize myself anymore.

Here at Maslow's very basic level of need, I became preoccupied with not having enough. As Eldar Shafir and Sendhil Mullainathan describe in their book on the topic, "Scarcity captures the mind. When we experience scarcity of any kind, we also become absorbed by it. . . . [Scarcity] changes how we think. It imposes itself on our minds."[4] Being constantly in need of basic necessities soon made everything else in my life, including school, secondary. Much later, when building my organization, this experience will significantly influence how we help young parents earn their college degrees. We will address their basic needs and their academic needs *equally*, understanding how all-consuming food insecurity or homelessness can be while trying to study for a test or answering a professor's email. The Hope Center for College, Community, and Justice will find in 2020 that more than 50 percent of college students with children experience food insecurity, and nearly 70 percent were housing insecure in the previous year. We will try to remove as many barriers to these supports as possible, recognizing that their time is precious and limited.

Another crucial building block in our model, gleaned from my own experience, will be relationships. People and the importance of a strong network will be at the very core of how we surround young families with resources—before logic models, data, technology—because during one of the most difficult and pivotal times in my life, it was *people* who made sure I graduated from high school.

One of those people was Tallwood's principal, Mr. Morgan, a round man in his fifties, with a thick mustache like Mario and Luigi, the plumber brothers from the Super Mario Bros. Nintendo game that Anika and I used to play. Despite Tallwood having two thousand students, he miraculously knew everyone's name. He was one of the few educators at Tallwood who seemed to genuinely *enjoy* students—all students. At the time, the fact that Mr. Morgan was a Black man leading a high school in Virginia in the '90s was lost on me. He was the first principal at Tallwood, Virginia Beach's newest high school, built on the plantation of William Nicholas, who came to Kempsville in 1642. Now I understand that his position, as a person of color, meant everything for me in that moment, as a pregnant Black girl.

Perhaps Mr. Morgan knew that Black girls are disproportionately disciplined in schools. In 2014, the African American Policy Forum and Columbia Law School's Center for Intersectionality and Social Policy Studies will find Black girls are nearly six times more likely to get an out-of-school suspension than their White peers and more likely to be suspended multiple times than any other gender or race of student—and this disproportionate discipline begins as early as preschool.[5] Or maybe he understood that for me, as a high school dropout, the consequences would be significant. As a Black girl, I would make less money than other white male or female high school dropouts, be more likely to need government assistance, and be at risk for poorer health outcomes. My child would also be more likely to drop out of high school than the children of other high school dropouts.[6]

It would take more than a decade for these numbers to surface and an awareness of the unique needs of Black girls to build momentum so it's more likely that Mr. Morgan was unaware of these facts. More plausible is that just by virtue of being a person of color in a leadership position, he was more patient, understanding, and concerned with my well-being than others might have been. When he looked at me, perhaps he saw his own daughter, wife, or mother. Black and Brown principals and educators were—and still are—few and far between, making it harder for girls of color, especially pregnant and parenting girls, to stay in school and succeed.

The day I told my mother about the baby, after leaving Mrs. Walker's room, I gravitated to the front office, where I asked to see Mr. Morgan. Before his assistant could tell me to go back to class, he emerged from his office with his familiar smile. It faded when he saw my red eyes and puffy face. He motioned for me to come inside. I blurted out that I was pregnant, and he let me cry into his brown suit jacket. We stood there like that until the sobbing subsided. Then he handed me a tissue and told me he would work things out with my teachers, and if I needed anything, to let him know. He also wrote a note so I could leave school early and drive to Mrs. Davis's house. She had been diagnosed with breast cancer, and our visits were important to us both now.

In those last few months of school, I needed Mr. Morgan. I didn't have money for prescriptions or transportation to the doctor, but when I had to get prenatal vitamins, he put a twenty in my hand and told me to go right to the pharmacy.

"Take my car," he'd say, throwing me the keys. "And pick up some donuts for the receptionists on your way back."

My guidance counselor, Mrs. Thornberry, was another support in her own quiet way. An older White woman who always wore bright floral dresses and skirts, she wasn't particularly warm, but she was consistent. We'd met a few times during my senior year to talk about my college plans, discuss which schools I'd apply to, and confirm that my SAT scores were meeting requirements. When she discovered my pregnancy, she called me into her office, looked at me through her red-rimmed glasses, and told me that she wanted to make sure I was still able to graduate with honors despite the drop in my GPA and attendance issues during my final grading period. She talked to all of my teachers, including my journalism teacher, and wrote an appeal so my absences wouldn't prevent me from graduating on time—which Mr. Morgan signed.

And even though Mrs. Davis was too sick to teach her special education classes, she was always a phone call away, telling me that everything would be okay.

Had these people not advocated for me, had they not been committed to my success and in positions with the power to remove barriers, my life would have turned out differently. My transition to college might have been delayed or not happened at all. So many young women, particularly women of color, who experience a pregnancy don't have advocates in the right places, people who see their promise and potential and fight for it. Efforts to help young parents overcome the obstacles of teen pregnancy must include building support systems that were never there before or repairing ones that were decimated by a pregnancy. They must include social capital in the form of champions and cheerleaders that are often constants for their non-parenting and more affluent peers.

· · · · ·

I stood in line waiting for my name to be called. The girl in front of me smiled nervously at me over her shoulder. I smiled back and then smoothed down my hair and the gold honors sash draped around my neck. The night before, Paula had straightened my curls for my big day, but the Virginia humidity caused it to frizz here and there. I heard Mr. Morgan eagerly call my name, his voice resonating throughout Virginia Beach Pavilion. People clapped and cheered all around me as I walked up the steps to meet him at the podium. I threw my arms open wide, and we hugged. He whispered something to me, but I couldn't hear it over the crowd.

This marked my first accomplishment in the storm, and it was necessary for every accomplishment that followed. Things had gone dark so quickly that I didn't know who I was anymore, and I started to doubt my ability to do what I used to consider simple things. College was always a given, but now, between not having food to eat and struggling to get to school every day, it seemed completely unattainable. I was almost embarrassed to talk or even think about it, the words feeling childish and delusional when they came out. Anyone could see that just graduating from high school was a shaky proposition, never mind college.

But here I was. Even through the many missteps, the emotional upheaval, the physical changes, the obstacles that seemed to come one right after the other, and the tattered support system, I graduated. I achieved what more than half of pregnant teens don't achieve for reasons I was now acutely aware of. That one victory made my plan of going to college with a baby feel a little less crazy. There was at least a *slim* chance that it was possible.

I learned then that progress is like a staircase, each triumph a necessary precursor to the next. Nija reinforced this when I asked her what made her want to go to college after becoming pregnant. She told me that maintaining a 3.0 GPA and graduating from high school while homeless and pregnant was transformative: "I had hope. My mindset started to change." Prior to her pregnancy, she didn't consider herself college material, but her ability to overcome insurmountable odds convinced her otherwise. We tell young people that their lives are over when they discover their pregnancies and scratch our heads when they don't succeed, but this is the time when we need to remind them of their strength, encourage them to soar, and give them the chance to hope.

My parents and Rakheim greeted me after the ceremony. We stood outside in the heat and took pictures with awkward and uneasy smiles that continued into our dinner at a seafood restaurant on the oceanfront. I was overcome by sadness as I watched them across the table trying to find the right words. They were like strangers now—so detached from my everyday struggles and my adult problems. I knew this day was bittersweet for them, its specialness overshadowed by all that had transpired. Yet they had played a significant part in my ability to even reach this milestone. They raised Anika and me to be fiercely independent and confident. They demanded excellence. They told us we could achieve anything as long as we worked hard for it. But now my future was uncertain, and they didn't even have the satisfaction of knowing where I rested my head each night.

That night, I was determined to feel like a normal teenager celebrating their high school graduation. Everyone was heading down to the oceanfront where we'd celebrated so many occasions—birthdays, Memorial

Day weekend, the first day of summer. I didn't drink or smoke, but I did my best to stay up and celebrate. It wasn't enough. Bree and the other girls soon grew bored of me and were ready to drop me off somewhere. Hours later, in the quiet of early morning, I walked into Tina's apartment. Rakheim was still on the strip with his friends. Tina was upstairs with her bedroom door closed, probably smoking weed or sleeping. I could hear a commercial advertising bathroom tile cleaner coming from her TV. I sat on the couch, slipped off my shoes, and didn't bother reaching for the light switch.

One thing made me lose everything.

Then I lost the baby.

CHAPTER 6

RED

CRIMSON-COLORED CLOUDS slowly turned the water red until the blood encircled me. I sat, shivering, in the bathtub, unsure of how much of this was normal—how much blood I was supposed to be losing—but I couldn't even gather my legs together and push up to stand. I could only rest my head back against the cold tiles and cry.

This pain was different from anything I'd ever felt. The process robs you of something you've been nurturing. It tells you that it's time. Forcefully, it woke up all the female parts inside of me that had been working silently over the past few months, first to form life and then to discard it. They were very much alive now, coming together to produce waves of pressure that flowed through my body until it seemed everything was out. Empty and aching, I wrapped myself in a towel, put on a pad, and went to bed.

The doctor had told me I would start spotting and soon the blood would become heavier. Then, he said, I would miscarry. Emotionless, he watched me as I sat on the edge of the examination table, my whole body shaking under my thin robe. I told him, through tears, that I didn't believe him. He went on to say that the miscarriage could have been a result of too much stress or my body just doing a "rehearsal" for a viable pregnancy later on. His robotic explanations weren't comforting. I didn't want to accept the fact that any of this was even happening.

Despite my pleading for him not to go, Rakheim was out of town with friends when I received this news. I felt completely alone. The word *miscarriage* was unfamiliar and confusing. No one talked about it. I assumed that if you got pregnant, nine months later, you would be holding a baby in your arms. The thought of complications and an early end to the pregnancy never crossed my mind. I would learn much later that 15 percent of all teenage pregnancies result in a miscarriage[1] and that so many women, young and old, lose babies every day. But then, at eighteen, I blamed myself for what seemed like a rare occurrence, so sure I must have done something wrong to make it happen—like not drinking enough water or eating enough vegetables. Other days, I blamed Rakheim for his fits of anger and long absences and the toll all of that probably took on my body. And in the midst of this, like many young women who experience a miscarriage, I was afraid to talk to anyone about my pain for fear of being shamed for mourning a life that wasn't supposed to exist in the first place.

The baby wasn't even a baby. After three months, its growth had slowed until eventually it was nothing more than tissue. There was no heartbeat. There was no life. Just as the doctor said, it began with a few drops of blood, and then in gushes, my body slowly began expelling a pregnancy gone wrong. I went back to his office, hoping that an ultrasound would reveal some opportunity to save it, but it only confirmed what would eventually happen in the bathtub. I'd been losing the pregnancy little by little. The one thing that had turned my life upside down was now disappearing.

I mourned for it until the soreness waned, and my body started to feel like itself again—no longer carrying life and no longer throbbing from the absence of it. Still, some days I missed the baby I had emotionally prepared for. It had thrown my life off course in every way, and now that it was gone, I wasn't sure what to do without it. Other days, I was happy to be Nicole again, to have control over my body, and to have a real chance at college again. I reasoned that just as God had sprung the pregnancy on me, he had similarly decided it wasn't the right time. There was a reason I became pregnant at seventeen, and there had to be a reason I miscarried, even if none of it made sense to me now. These assurances gave me the strength to get out of bed every morning and to eventually find peace.

Rakheim, who was everything to me now—mother, father, best friend—held me while I cried. He was similarly confused and devastated, blaming the doctor for not doing more to save our baby. When we got to a point where we could talk about moving forward, he said he wanted to try to get pregnant again, even though we had nothing. No home. No money.

I was learning to accept this cataclysmic existence as my new normal, including the miscarriage. Each day was an upheaval, whether it was financial, relational, or logistical. Nothing was guaranteed—not breakfast, not Rakheim coming home at night, not clean clothes, not a baby, and not our living situation. I spent the first few minutes of every morning in bed bracing myself for what might go wrong that day and trying to mentally get ahead of it. Keeping the dream of going to college alive through all of this was mentally exhausting.

Even with this uncertainty and losing the baby, I didn't want to go home. Home still felt worse than being on this roller coaster with Rakheim. We left Yvonne and Sharon's shortly after graduation and slept in a school parking lot in the back seat of Tina's car. That was something we did often, whenever we couldn't secure a place to stay. In the morning, Rakheim called Tina from Hardee's, where we stopped to get breakfast, and convinced her to let us sleep on her floor until we found something more permanent.

Tina, like others, thought I was getting in the way of Rakheim's football career, and stunting him from making something of himself. I couldn't believe how wrong so many people could be about me and about our situation. No one wanted Rakheim to succeed more than I did, but people considered my pregnancy a scheme and a trap to keep him in a relationship, and the miscarriage made them question if I was ever even pregnant. The reality was that schools stopped reaching out to Rakheim once they found out his GPA was so low he was in jeopardy of not even graduating from high school. For a long time, his focus and energy had been on selling and being with his friends rather than football and school. His prospects and stardom were fading.

We stayed with Tina for a couple of weeks until Rakheim found a room for rent in an old house in Norfolk. His friend's mom owned the property, which was built by her grandfather in the 1940s, and agreed to let us pay $250 a month. Any excitement I might have had about having our own place disappeared when we pulled up to the small, dilapidated house. The house was condemned, except for two rooms at the top of a lopsided staircase. You had to skip some of the steps to prevent yourself from falling through. Our bedroom was decent, just white walls, bright green carpet, and a small closet in the corner. Three windows allowed some light in and looked down on the street below. We put a microwave on top of the TV because none of the appliances worked downstairs in the neglected kitchen.

My parents were in the process of relocating to Alexandria, a suburb of DC, where they'd bought a townhouse closer to my dad's job. Mom said we could take some of the things they were planning to get rid of, including a queen-sized bed, bookshelves, and a set of dishes, as well as the things I'd left in my room. I agreed to come by and pick up some items.

The drive back to my old neighborhood was difficult, stirring up memories of a time when life was easier and my future seemed certain. We passed Jay's Wings, the dry cleaner where my dad took his suits for work, and the Applebee's we frequented for dinners out as a family. While landmarks of my former life flashed by, I shifted toward the window in the Cadillac's cavernous, gray leather seat to hide my glassy eyes from Rakheim. He wouldn't understand. I always said I never wanted to go back, but the familiar streets reminded me of how things were before the pregnancy, and it was so different from my current reality—a condemned house, a drug-dealing boyfriend, and a constant loneliness.

My mom opened the door in a black T-shirt and blue jeans that were colored with smudges of oil paint, and with a sadness in her face that surprised me. She forced a smile, her chin quivering. We hadn't seen each other since my graduation, and it must have been overwhelming to have me standing on her front step again. Just as I'd felt during the drive back home, it must have reminded her of a simpler time when I was just a senior in high school preparing to head off to college. When I first left, I pictured her spending most of her nights up worrying about me, wondering where I was and if I was okay, but by now, I thought she'd be used to my absence. I thought time would make things easier. Now I know that, for a mother, being estranged from a child can feel like a fresh wound no matter how much time has passed.

She watched us as we worked and finally broke the silence by asking me about the baby. I dragged a trash bag full of clothes past her into the hallway and said over my shoulder, flatly, that I had miscarried. I could hear her breath tremble. I knew there were probably tears in her eyes, but I was so angry at everything that I couldn't stop to look at her, and I didn't have the words to talk about it.

· · · · ·

I tried to make our room in the broken-down house feel like a home. I put a few pictures on the walls and kept things clean and organized. I prepared our dinners in the microwave on top of the TV, mostly pizzas and Hot Pockets. Rakheim eventually bought a portable electric burner that we plugged in to make grilled cheese sandwiches and Steak-umms. I stacked the white dishes from my parents' house on my old bookshelf and washed them in the hallway bathroom sink while listening to CDs on my old stereo. I sang along to Mary J. and rapped to Lil' Kim as I worked, the old floorboards creaking and straining underneath my feet.

More and more, Rakheim left me at the house alone. Early in the morning, I'd hear the faint horn of a car outside on the street below, and he'd roll out of bed, pull on his clothes, then kiss my cheek, and close the door behind him. As the morning light shifted around the room to an afternoon glare and then dissolved into night, I sat there without a phone, money, sometimes food to eat, or a way to leave. I spent most of my time trying to catch a signal on our TV antenna and rearranging our things while waiting for him to return. After I saw a rat running around the perimeter of the room, I refused to get up from the bed unless Rakheim was home with me. I was paralyzed and completely dependent on him. As hard as it was to live like that, there was something romantic about the two of us making something out of nothing just so we could be together.

Rakheim and I were similarly feeling the isolating effects of poverty, but each day held different experiences for the two of us that summer. I was oblivious to anything happening outside of the walls of our tiny room—Japan's trip to Mars, the instant movie classic *Saving Private Ryan*, or the details of the Monica Lewinsky and President Clinton scandal. Rakheim's world consisted of different street corners and motel rooms, a constant roller coaster of cars, people, police, and drugs. This was the start of a wedge that would form and grow between us over the next two years, beginning with leading different lives and fed by constant financial and communication issues. We would never walk down the aisle, despite his musings that one day we'd be married. Our fate would reflect the outcome for most young parents; less than 8 percent marry within a year after their child is born.[2]

On the rare occasions when he was home, we spent most of our time fighting. I'd beg for him to get a real job, even if it was at McDonald's. I didn't care what it was as long as he was making an honest living and coming home to me. His response was always the same: he'd never make enough money to support us earning Virginia's $5.15 minimum wage, and he refused to flip burgers. I interpreted this refusal as an affront—a choice of the streets over me and our life together. Our clashes would be so extreme that we'd break furniture or turn over the mattress. We argued so much and so intensely that it scared me. In the end, we'd retreat to separate sides of the room out of breath.

"I don't want to live like this," I told him.

"I know, boo." He ran his hand through his dreadlocks. "Just give me some time."

But time never made any difference. It didn't fix anything. We were always broke, I was always alone, he was always gone, and the drug dealing didn't stop. The constant repairs for his Cadillac sucked up the $1,500 I had in savings from my time working at Kmart. We barely made rent each month. There were nights when he came home from a day of selling with only seventy cents in his pocket—just enough to buy a two-liter of ginger ale from the over-priced 7-Eleven, which was our only real source of food supplies, up the street. We'd drink that for a day or two to ward off hunger. Other times, I'd feel his hand on my back in the early morning and hear him whisper, "Guess what baby? Today was a good day," presenting me with a takeout box of pancakes, bacon, and eggs from IHOP. The pride in his face made it impossible for me to tell him how miserable I was.

I decided to get a job. First, I worked at City Lights, an eighteen-and-up club that we used to go to in high school, around the corner from the house on Clovel. The owner, an older White man with a red mullet and an endless supply of black leather vests and cowboy boots, offered to hire me when I went there one night with Rakheim. My job was easy—sit at the door and put ID bracelets on anyone over twenty-one. It felt good to have income and a purpose to each day again, even something as small as securing neon yellow strips around people's wrists and collecting their cover charge. I liked having people to talk to again. I'd sit on my stool just inside the door and joke and laugh with the bouncers, who were like big brothers, stepping in whenever a guy got too close to me. Rakheim hated the idea of me being "eye candy" though. He was happy when I got fired for not showing up for work one night because he'd gotten arrested for driving on a suspended license, and I was too busy driving around with Tina to pull together bail money.

My next job came from a search through the classifieds in a newspaper we bought from 7-Eleven. I answered the ad, which claimed to be looking for "managers" and promised that you could be running your own "operation" within six months. I had no idea what the product was or what I would be managing, but I was attracted to the prospect of quick money. Sitting in a room with twenty other people, I found out in the open-call interview that the product was generic designer fragrances. Later I would realize that the company, Continental Industries, was a pyramid scheme promising big payoffs and lavish trips that none of us would ever see. Instead, we'd spend months peddling a bag full of copycat fragrances and getting paid a slim percentage of the sales in cash under the table. The enterprise preyed on people like me who had limited options.

Rakheim was similarly excited about the promise of fast cash. He borrowed Tina's car every morning to drop me off at the office park right off of Virginia Beach Boulevard for the two-week training. Each day, I had to shadow a couple of salespeople in preparation for approaching potential customers on my own. During hot summer days, we'd go to gas stations, strip malls, and parking lots, pitching to anyone who looked like they might be open to a conversation. So as not to saturate the local market, we made weekend trips to nearby areas like North Carolina or rural Virginia. I was amazed by how many bottles of perfume the advanced salespeople could push in one day—sometimes thirty or forty.

"Can I ask you a question? What kind of perfume or cologne do you wear?" That's how we'd try to start the conversation. Some people would just ignore you and walk away, but a good number of people would answer, and the sale would unfold from there.

My training class dwindled to only ten people. Those who left were discouraged by the two-dollar-per-bottle commission and the countless hours on our feet. The rest of us were so desperate for this to work that we stayed. When we came back to the office after a long day of sales, Tony, the manager, greeted us with high fives, but I teetered between wanting to impress him and not trusting him. He seemed as authentic to me as his spray-on orange tan and his rehearsed pep talks. If you didn't hit your numbers, he humiliated you in front of everyone and questioned your drive. Not only did the job pay poorly—I averaged sixty dollars per week—but it was also highly competitive and deflating.

I felt stuck. Our finances were so tight that even this little amount of money was critical. No matter how much I wanted to, I couldn't quit, and there weren't many other options, especially with unreliable transportation and only a high school diploma. If I wasn't selling fake perfume, I'd be working at a department store, making fast food, or cleaning toilets. I was getting a small taste of the scarcity, sacrifice, and limited options that many of my future students lived with their entire lives. When Yoslin tells me her story years later, it will take me back to this time of desperation—a brief episode for me compared to her entire life.

Yoslin arrived in the US from El Salvador when she was nine years old with her younger sister and her pregnant mother. While her mother worked three jobs to support the family, it wasn't enough. As a third grader, Yoslin woke up early on Sunday mornings to cook tortillas, pupusas, enchiladas, and empanadas and spent the day selling them to people in her apartment complex or at a nearby soccer field. "I would usually sell four hundred dollars' worth and that would help my mom pay the bills," she will tell me. Her mom had two more children, creating a greater need, so at thirteen, Yoslin began working with her grandfather as a janitor at night to bring in more money. She was able to secure her Deferred Action for Childhood Arrivals (DACA) status at fifteen, which gave her limited deportation protection and a work permit. With DACA, she could work full-time at McDonald's every day after school, from 3 p.m. to 11 p.m., turning over her entire paycheck to her mother each week. At sixteen, she became pregnant, and by the time I met her, when she was accepted into our program, she was a married mother of two, an aspiring public policy major at a community college, and a janitor working the night shift.

"I didn't really have a childhood," she will tell me. "I had to grow up too quick."

Young parents like Yoslin, who began working at nine years old, when most of us were still playing with action figures and Barbie dolls, will be among the most hardworking people I will ever meet, juggling multiple jobs that pay very little with school and parenting or waking up in shelters to get themselves and their kids ready for classes and work. This is the reality, but it is shrouded and overpowered by the pervasive notion that teen parents—like everyone living in poverty—are lazy. In 2004, on the nationally syndicated broadcast of *The Radio Factor*, Bill O'Reilly will say this about poor people: "You gotta look people in the eye and tell 'em they're irresponsible and lazy. And who's gonna wanna do that? Because that's what poverty is, ladies and gentlemen." It is jarring but revealing that, in 2016, the Bureau of Labor Statistics will report that roughly 7.6 million Americans make up the "working poor," people who live below the poverty line but spend at least half the year either working or looking for employment. It is why so many people who are or were teen parents find their prospects for upward mobility stifled at every turn.

Maybe Rakheim was inspired by me getting up every day for work or by my constant nagging. Either way, he got a job at a carpentry shop in the same office park as Continental Industries. He told me when he picked me up from work one day, and I threw my arms around him and kissed him all over his face, unable to contain my happiness. It felt like things were slowly coming together. We had a roof over our heads and some steady income. He could stop selling drugs, and I could start reapplying to college. We could have a normal life.

. . . . .

In order for my plan to come together, the Cadillac *had* to be working. There was no other way to make it to the doctor without Rakheim knowing. Tina never let me use her car, and I didn't have any friends to give me a ride. I'd been mapping all of this out in my head for weeks, strategizing and calculating the probability of each component falling into place. I walked across a Hecht's parking lot one July afternoon, with my duffel bag of perfume, and found a pay phone to call the doctor's office and make an appointment, knowing there was a good chance I would never make it. But amazingly, when the day came, the Cadillac was working, and I was able to convince Rakheim to let me use it to run to the grocery store. With just enough time to head down I-64 toward the office, I grabbed the keys off of the floor while he took a nap.

The baby-blue cushioned chairs, the skylights above, and even the receptionist with her brown hair neatly pulled up into a bun all reminded me of being pregnant and the anticipation I used to have in that office, but today's visit was about something completely different. It was about *preventing* a baby. I had decided to start taking birth control pills. Now that Rakheim and I had jobs, and there was a real possibility that I could go to college, this decision was my first step back in the right direction. I was feeling older and wiser now, after a few months of being on my own, and protecting myself from a pregnancy was about reclaiming my control and my future.

As rational as this sounded, it had to be a secret, like so many secrets that seemed to be accumulating between Rakheim and me. Losing the baby felt like I was being given a second chance, but he wouldn't understand that. He'd consider birth control a betrayal since after the miscarriage, we spent so many nights talking about trying to have another baby. At first, my grief made me want to try, too, but eventually, knowing how unprepared we were and how difficult life would be, that desire faded. I tried to hint at waiting to get pregnant again so I could instead focus on my education, but he'd snap at me or quickly change the subject. Just thinking about how explosive his reaction would be if he knew I was sitting in that office made me want to get back in the car and drive to the grocery store.

I won't learn that this fear has a name until I'm much older. Reproductive coercion involves a partner hindering contraception, pressuring a woman to become pregnant, or physically or sexually abusing her or threatening to leave if she doesn't become pregnant. It's often less about a partner wanting to settle down or start a family and more about them wanting complete and long-lasting control, which I would come to learn was Rakheim's ultimate goal. Seeing this in the arduous situations of several of my program's students, whose children were the results of this coercion or who needed help escaping relationships in which this coercion was happening, will crystallize the foggy dynamics between Rakheim and me. It will also confirm the complexities of teen pregnancy and challenge our assumptions about how and why young women become pregnant.

In 2007, an assistant professor of pediatrics at the University of California, Davis, School of Medicine will interview sixty-one girls from Boston's poorest neighborhoods—all with varying racial and ethnic backgrounds but with histories of intimate-partner violence. The study will reveal how pervasive reproductive coercion is for teen girls; more than half of the girls were in abusive and sexually active relationships at the time of the study, and of those girls, 26 percent will say that their partners were "actively trying to get them pregnant." Another study, released in 2019, will survey 550 sexually active females between the ages of fourteen and nineteen years old, who received care at school health centers in northern California in 2012 or 2013, finding that "almost one in eight teen girls reported a partner recently tried to coerce her to become pregnant."[3]

Before I could gather my things and head back to the car, the nurse called my name, startling me out of my thoughts. I stood up and followed her back to an exam room.

The next morning, I took the first little pink pill in the hallway bathroom with a gulp of water from the faucet and held a hand over my mouth so Rakheim wouldn't hear me cry. I was crying about lying. I was crying about not having a baby. I was crying about not knowing where to hide the pack of pills in our tiny room.

CHAPTER 7

PLACE

LIKE A MASSIVE SHIP, it carried me in and out of cities and along the seam of the thick woods to the newest place—not *my* place—just the newest one. I was learning to live without a place, to anchor myself to nothing and no one. I was no longer attached to a room or belongings or even people. The past few months had taught me how fragile those things were and how painful losing them could be. The safest way to function was to simply let them go.

When the bus left the Granby Street Greyhound Station in a slow push, its engine groaned, and through the cloud of gray smoke exploding from the back, I could see Rakheim, standing in the cold below with his hand still raised in a goodbye. His sad eyes followed the bus as we turned the corner and disappeared. It was December 1998. I was eighteen years old, and despite being on the pill, I was four months pregnant. The doctor had prescribed combination birth control pills, which require backup contraception for a week, and we conceived some time in those first seven days. Like many young women sitting in doctors' offices and clinics, I never received this warning or information on long-acting methods, such as an intrauterine device (IUD) or an injectable contraceptive, that are often more successful than the pill. Depo-Provera and Norplant were introduced in the early '90s giving teens access to more effective methods and were largely responsible for the steady decline of the teen pregnancy rate that decade. When I got pregnant, the rates were actually at their lowest in twenty years—down 19 percent, from 117 pregnancies per 1,000 women ages fifteen to nineteen in 1990 to 93 per 1,000 in 1997.[1]

But I will be almost thirty years old, married, with two degrees, by the time I finally learn what an IUD is from a midwife after the birth of my second child. She will carefully walk me through my options, answer my questions, and laugh with me through the triumphs and frustrations of having a newborn. My brief, transactional, and awkward interactions with health professionals as a teen will give me a special appreciation for the midwife relationship—and will help me understand how thorough medical information is a luxury for young women, particularly for Black and Brown girls. Hearing story after story from young mothers in my program who became pregnant while on birth control or because they couldn't obtain birth control will solidify for me the inextricable link between teen pregnancy and ingrained racism in our healthcare system.

In high school, I wrote a three-page double-spaced paper on Margaret Sanger for health class, providing me with a very cursory understanding of her work and the history of reproductive health in the US. I focused only on Sanger opening the first birth-control clinic in the United States in 1916 based on her beliefs that birth control is a fundamental women's right and that efforts by the church and government to suppress it are actually efforts to suppress a woman's personal freedom. My quick online search and a thumb through of a few library books didn't reveal that Sanger's legacy is marred by her use of eugenic language popular in the early twentieth century that promoted the idea of selective breeding to improve the human race. Language that, her critics say, often focused on limiting births in the Black community. It also didn't reveal the counterargument from her staunch supporters that Sanger was simply advocating for the reproductive rights of Black women who were—and still are—particularly exposed to the impacts of unplanned pregnancy because their birth control was—and still is—so limited by poverty and a discriminatory health care system. I will later discover that Sanger wasn't the only prominent figure in the eugenics movement. People attached to popular household brands that we use today were champions, too, like Dr. Clarence Gamble, heir to the Procter & Gamble fortune, and James Hanes, the hosiery tycoon.

If, as a sophomore in high school, I had stumbled upon eugenics and its connection to extreme acts of exclusion and prejudice against women of color who were trying to access quality healthcare, I might have dismissed it as a far-fetched conspiracy theory. My own subtle exclusions and daily work in the contradictions of teen pregnancy much later will encourage me to actively seek out this history and context. I will learn that, shrouded in fancy words about eliminating social ills and backed by wealthy supporters, the eugenics movement led to government sterilization programs in thirty-one states that targeted marginalized populations. More than thirty thousand people in prisons or psychiatric institutions in twenty-nine states were sterilized, without their knowledge or consent, in the early 1900s. By the 1960s, these programs sterilized tens of thousands more, beyond the mentally ill or incarcerated.[2] Elaine Riddick, a Black thirteen-year-old girl who was raped by her neighbor in Winfall, North Carolina, in 1967, was one of them. A five-person state eugenics board in Raleigh decided that, because of her poor academic performance and "promiscuity," doctors should immediately cut and tie her fallopian tubes without her consent as soon as she gave birth.[3] She didn't realize what had happened to her until years later, when she and her husband wanted to have more children and a doctor told her she'd been "butchered." It won't be until 2003, the year I will graduate from college with my daughter by my side, that North Carolina will finally repeal its involuntary sterilization law.

Numerous other states were guilty of these practices. Some 30 percent of women in Puerto Rico were unable to have children by 1965—a result of a sterilization campaign on the island that began shortly after World War I, when the governor declared a job shortage and overpopulation.[4] The US government forced the sterilization of thousands of Native American women between 1970 and 1976, singling out "full-blooded Indian women," resulting in as many as 25 to 50 percent of Native American women being robbed of their ability to have children.[5] California performed more government-funded sterilizations than any other state—a third of all procedures in the United States—largely on Latinx and Blacks. In many cases, these women were under twenty-one, like Elaine; some were as young as nine years old.

Decades after writing my paper on Sanger, and working with hundreds of young mothers, I will be frustrated by the bias that is baked into our healthcare system and continues to leave women—particularly young women of color—in the dark about their reproductive health and rights. The healthcare system provides these women with little information about what is happening to their bodies, offers limited birth control options, and pushes, even forces, cesarean as opposed to vaginal births. I will learn that mistakes made during medical procedures go without explanations, sometimes without acknowledgment. These are some of the dire consequences of bias. I will discover that most people's understanding of how pervasive these problems will be is similar to my level of understanding as a sophomore in high school, that they also consider it distant history and not particularly relevant to the issue of teen pregnancy. Most will not know about or make a connection between the mistreatment of Black and Brown women by the medical field when hearing that women of color are less likely to use effective, long-acting methods of contraception, such as hormonal methods and IUDs, and that this trend is more concentrated among younger women.[6]

The slight curve of my belly barely revealed a pregnancy, but over those four months, my daughter was taking shape inside of me. Her sweet nose and soft lips were starting to form, and even though I couldn't feel it, she was flexing her arms and legs and clasping her little hands into fists. Later, when I am pregnant with my other children, I will know how important it is to read and sing to them while they're in utero. I will read every prenatal book I can find and eagerly await my weekly pregnancy emails filled with information about my changing body and what an unborn baby needs. But as a young mother with more stress than time or resources, most of what this child heard of the outside world were voices raised in anger.

Even though he'd promised he would stop, the carpentry job didn't replace Rakheim's drug dealing. I found out one night when the sound of rocks hitting our window stirred me out of our sleep. Through a squinted eye, I watched him go to the window, open it, and in an angry whisper, tell a man in the front yard that he'd be down in a minute. Then he found his pants on the floor and fished around in his pocket for the small yellow crystals wrapped tightly in a thin layer of plastic. Using only the moonlight to see, he sat on the side of the bed and divided out a small piece for the man, then quickly looked at me before opening the door and going downstairs.

With the morning came one of our many fights, the kind the whole street could hear. It felt like pregnancy just intensified all of my anger, my passion, and my mounting frustrations. I was in love with someone I'd always been taught to stay away from, but when each face-off ended, he could be so fragile, sometimes crying in my lap, saying God had forgotten about him. The star athlete who exuded confidence when we talked on the bleachers at Tallwood was gone, and the person he left behind was often unrecognizable. There was no grand plan for his future. Big dreams were replaced by deceptions. He was obsessed with selling and so money-hungry that he couldn't see how poor we really were. I tried to convince myself that there was still a flicker of the fire that used to propel him down the football field, but each day, he proved me wrong.

Later, when my daughter is a little girl, she will have fits of anger so intense that I will sit alone in my room and cry, blaming myself for the turmoil of my pregnancy that she likely absorbed like the amniotic fluid that cushioned and sustained her. My fears will be shared by so many young mothers who remember the stress and trauma they experienced during their pregnancies and worry about the effects—like Chelsea and Kathy, who were beaten or choked during their pregnancies, or Ana, who was abandoned by the father of her child when she revealed she was expecting. I'll talk to others whose pregnancies were plagued by arguing, fighting, and isolation, like mine. And on top of all of this is the strain of a *teen* pregnancy. Our intuition will be confirmed by research showing the correlation between a mother's stress level and her child's growth and development.

A 2011 study in the *Journal of Child Psychology and Psychiatry* will find that infants who are exposed to higher levels of cortisol, a hormone released into the womb when mothers are stressed, have higher spikes in their own cortisol when their blood is drawn on the first day of life. They are literally born with heightened levels of stress. Four years later, in 2015, another study by researchers at the University of Notre Dame Australia and the Telethon Kids Institute will find that the children born to mothers who experienced three or more stressful events during pregnancy scored lower on motor-skills tests as teenagers than the children of mothers who experienced fewer than three stressful events. In other words, a mother's stress levels while pregnant can determine her child's coordination and motor-skills development into adolescence. For teen mothers, who are more likely to be poor, dealing with mental health issues, and in toxic relationships, stress is often inevitable. For their children, the hard work of overcoming the effects of this stress begins before they're even born. We expend so much energy and so many resources on figuring out how to help children living in poverty succeed with the notion that we can somehow address their needs separate from their mothers' when the two are—and always were—indivisible.

Tropical storms in coastal Virginia could be intense, but that August, Hurricane Bonnie was the most significant storm since 1960 with 90 mph winds and four to seven inches of rain. The night it hit, Rakheim went out to get a pack of Newports, a trip that would last well into the morning. While the thunder and rain beat against the windows, I searched for a signal on the TV until, eventually, the power went out. I stood at the window and watched the wind shake the trees and blow the toys around in circles in the yards below until a bolt of lightning seemed to light up the whole house. Then, I changed into one of Rakheim's T-shirts and fell asleep.

When I woke up, he wasn't beside me. A sound like an explosion had shaken me out of my sleep, and a smell like paint, cement, and wet wood all mixed together filled the room. It was dark, but above me I could discern a gaping hole in the ceiling a few inches to the left of the bed. Water began to drip in a slow, steady rhythm, soon meshing with the hammering rain outside. I was scared of what I might be inhaling and what I couldn't see—like rats waiting to drop down through the hole. I thought sleeping would be a better way to get through the night than sitting there, afraid, so I forced my eyes closed, moved as close as I could to the wall, and fell back asleep.

Rakheim called the landlord from a pay phone at 7-Eleven the next day, and she said she'd get the ceiling fixed in a few days, but after a week, the hole was still there. We tried to maneuver around it and the growing stench, but we knew it wasn't good for me or the baby. We figured if we didn't pay rent that month, she'd be forced to fix the ceiling, but one night, we came home from work to find that rather than making the repairs, she had changed the locks. In a heated exchange, she said we could get into the room and get our belongings when she got her money. Rakheim refused to pay, so we went back to sleeping on Tina's floor, and for two weeks, we wore the clothes we had on when we'd discovered the changed locks and the one or two outfits we found in the trunk of the Cadillac. The only shoes I had, brown clogs, were so tattered from walking endlessly selling perfume each day that each sole had a hole in it. While I stood in parking lots waiting for my next sale, I watched people and wondered if they knew how fortunate they were to have cars, homes, food in their stomachs, and good sturdy shoes.

Finally, the landlord agreed to let Rakheim back into the room to get some of our clothes. She stood over him as he packed a large trash bag full of shoes and clothes and a few photo albums, but that was it. She told him we couldn't get anything else in the room until we paid her the rent. I never saw the rest of those things again.

It's expensive to be poor: low-paying, physically taxing jobs; no car, or cars that need constant, costly repairs; food deserts that cause you to rely on fast food; and housing exploitation. Turns out, I was partially right when, as a child, I believed that housing is assigned to us. If you're poor, you're stuck in a cycle of substandard housing and housing insecurity that can last for generations. A year after we lost the room on Clovel, a University of Tennessee study found that the children of people who own their homes are more likely to finish high school (and twice as likely to graduate from college), and they are nearly 60 percent more likely to become homeowners themselves. In other words, housing is almost pre-determined—or assigned—by your parents' socioeconomic status. This presents a bleak outlook for young parents who are less likely to own homes or live in affluent neighborhoods, no matter how hard they work.

When a young mother *is* able to secure a place, she will likely experience housing exploitation, particularly if she is Black or Hispanic or Latinx. It involves landlords charging poor renters a higher rate than renters living in wealthier neighborhoods. On Clovel, in the middle of low-income, government housing, Rakheim and I were paying $250 a month for a room in a condemned house, which may have been a quarter of the property's worth in rent each month. Fifteen minutes away, at the Waterfront in downtown Norfolk's high-priced apartments, more affluent renters might have paid just a tenth of the property's value in rent each month. In addition to higher rent, exploitation includes "slumlords" forcing low-income renters to live in poor conditions, like holes in the ceiling they refuse to fix, or locking them out of their homes when they are late paying rent.

The room on Clovel was falling apart, unsafe, and rat-infested, but it was our home, and I was committed to making it our place in the world. In the end, though, despite our best efforts, we couldn't hold on to it, and losing it felt like losing everything—like losing more than just what *was* but also losing all that *could be*. Sociologist Matthew Desmond will capture this feeling in his book *Evicted*, in 2017, which follows eight families in Milwaukee in their quest for stable housing: "America is supposed to be a place where you can better yourself, your family, and your community. But this is only possible if you have a stable home." Young, pregnant, and homeless, I couldn't even keep a roof over my head. How could I conceive of something as ambitious as going to college?

· · · · ·

Fall arrived and with it, the cool air and the moms buttoning up their children's jackets and stuffing tissues in their pockets for runny noses. The red and orange hues that lined the streets reminded me of the autumns back in New England when I used to stand at the top of our street and look down at the changing colors of the trees. The bright leaves overpowered the road—vibrant and alive, like my mother's paint palette. The lavenders were my favorite.

I watched all of this through the window of my coworker's apartment, where Rakheim and I had been sleeping for weeks in blankets on her living room floor. I knew that the change in season also meant my high school friends were well into their first semester of college, making lifelong connections, cheering at football games, discovering themselves, paving their own paths, and I was here, standing still. I was disconnected, and I felt it. Soon, I would quit selling perfume and be among the roughly 14 percent of young people between sixteen and twenty-four who were not in school or working that year—along with Rakheim.[7] Our disconnection pushed us to the margins, no longer linked to a pathway of opportunity that would allow us to build toward something or lay any foundation for our future. No more lifeline to advocates like football coaches, choir directors, counselors, or teachers. Even Mrs. Davis felt distant during our infrequent phone calls. By 2010, the rate of disconnected youth will increase to nearly 15 percent.

While we often identify pregnancy as the reason for their disconnection because it's such an easy target, half of teen mothers drop out of school *before* becoming pregnant.[8] That's because disconnection transcends being enrolled in school or earning an hourly wage. One of the top questions I will get after each of my talks as an activist and speaker will be how, as a teen with so much promise and a clear path to college, I became pregnant. While the answer is packed and complex, I can trace it back to its earliest manifestations in a father who was physically present but emotionally absent. Others, like Rakheim, will feel the vast gulf of a parent or both parents who are absent physically and emotionally. When we think about the number of young people who are disconnected from the adults in their lives—from the people who validate their worth and who can help them reach their goals—the number of disconnected sixteen- to twenty-four-year-olds likely soars well above 15 percent, and the effects can be tragic. More than two decades later, convinced that connection is one of the most important components of any successful social intervention, I will secure an enlarged Mother Teresa quote to the conference room wall of our DC office that reads "We think sometimes that poverty is only being hungry, naked and homeless. The poverty of being unwanted, unloved and uncared for is the greatest poverty."

I had a bladder infection, which is how I ended up on that Greyhound bus. It could have been caused by a lot of things, but in general, the doctor didn't think I was taking care of myself. While Rakheim stopped showing up for work at the carpentry shop and was exclusively selling again, I hung onto the perfume job, hoping it would pay off. When we made out-of-town sales trips, that meant days on my feet, more fast food, and sometimes staying in strip-mall parking lots pushing bottles until 10:30 at night. Sleeping on the floor made my back hurt, partly because of the growing baby and partly because of the hard surface. My appetite was sporadic. Sometimes the thought of food made me nauseous;

other times, I wanted a five-course meal. Unfortunately, we didn't have enough money to even buy groceries so I wasn't gaining weight like I was supposed to. My health teacher's presentation on teen mothers having tiny babies made more sense now. Not ingesting proper nutrients during pregnancy and limited access to prenatal care put us at a higher risk of preterm birth and a low-birth-weight baby. My inability to keep myself and this baby healthy felt like yet another failure.

When my mother asked me to come stay with her and my dad for a couple of months to get healthy, I said yes. As much as I didn't want to leave Rakheim, I was tired, I missed her, and I was also finally ready to quit the perfume scheme. Rakheim reluctantly agreed that living place-to-place, eating whatever we could find, and sleeping on people's floors wasn't good for me and the baby. We decided I'd stay with my parents for six weeks to rest and eat well. In the meantime, he promised he would save up some money and find us a real apartment to bring the baby home to. In the midst of the chaos, we had gotten him into the Apprentice School at Newport News Shipbuilding, where he'd be playing Division III football and studying to be a welder. One of the coaches there said they'd help us find a place to live.

The bus veered off of I-64 onto the long stretch of I-95. A mother and daughter sat across the aisle. The little girl slept peacefully in the perfect curve of her mother's side, two red bows at the end of her neatly woven braids on either side of her head. I thought about my mom crying in my arms when I told her about my first pregnancy. I thought about what going back home, even for a short time, would mean. Arguments. Anger. Tears. I eased my grip on the duffel bag in my lap and looked down at my hands. They were shaking.

It took six hours to get to the Greyhound station in a strip mall in Springfield, Virginia. When we emptied into the waiting area, I found a seat and read a magazine while waiting for my mom to walk through the door. My hands stopped shaking when she appeared in front of me, greeting me with her soft hazel eyes.

I slept on a futon in a small guest room that doubled as my mother's art studio. It was crowded by her bookshelves, stocked with her familiar art books, a computer desk, and a workspace underneath a large lamp where she did most of her drawing. Her sketches and inspirational photos of flowers and patron saints were taped to the walls around the room. The futon, with its wooden frame and cushioned mattress, was slightly more comfortable than the floors and the back seats of cars that I'd grown accustomed to sleeping on. What was most comforting, though, was the soothing quiet and having the space to just be in my own skin. This was not my space, and the fragility of the relationships in the house prevented it from being completely reliable, but the quiet brought a peacefulness that I hadn't experienced in a long time. I needed it for myself, and I needed it for the little life I was trying to grow. I needed it for dreaming again—imagining what those branches might be stretching and reaching for high up in the sky.

·····

Coming home was painful. My belly was small, but all of the tension I was experiencing made me feel like it was the size of a beach ball. I couldn't hide it. I couldn't pretend it didn't exist or try to minimize it. I felt like I was carrying the weight of my decisions. My mom, the artist, was in overdrive, trying to mend and fix our family, even though we'd been breaking for a long time. My dad spent most of his time in his office absorbed in his work, or downstairs comforted by the melodies of Ella Fitzgerald or Sarah Vaughan. He hardly looked at me or talked to me, except for his frequent lectures, each one emotional and tearful, each one involving him wanting me to understand how much I'd put my parents through and me apologizing. This familiar dance of constant yelling and crying with little resolve thrust me back to my childhood and all of its confusion and doubt. Just the setting, the new twitch in my father's cheek when he got really upset, and the way he now stuttered until he found the right words to say were different. Each night, I'd retreat to the futon, praying for God to help me feel good about myself again. The overpowering sadness scared me.

As we waited for the ball drop, I glanced at the phone in the kitchen, hoping it would ring, and Rakheim would be on the other end to wish me a happy New Year. He never called. I didn't hear from him until two days later. He called collect, which my father announced with a frown when he came into the guest room to tell me that Rakheim was on the phone. I slammed the book I was reading shut and ran into my parents' bedroom to take the call. The conversation didn't go well, mostly because his excuse for not calling on New Year's was that he was at City Lights, drunk, and had blown six hundred dollars at the bar, buying drinks for all of his friends. The amount was too much for me to even stomach. I bent over and cried into my knees. When he heard me crying, he told me he was sorry. He said he "fucked up" and would make it right.

The frustration gave me a moment of complete clarity. I calmly told him that if he hadn't secured the apartment for us by January 15, I wasn't coming home. I was prepared to stay with my parents because this baby needed a real home. Not expecting the ultimatum, he told me he may not have an apartment by then, but he had just met a new addict, Stacey, who would let us stay with her in Virginia Beach. I cut him short and told him I wasn't sleeping on people's floors anymore. If he didn't have the apartment, I wasn't coming home.

He said okay. He promised.

· · · · ·

The pulsing cursor on the screen reminded me of each second that passed without a word on the blank, white document. The assignment was clear—explain what I'd been doing for the last six months while out of school and why I wanted to reapply to the College of William & Mary—but how to answer it was not. This essay was necessary if I wanted to reopen my acceptance to the college. I sat at my dad's computer, with a pillow behind my back to cushion the growing ache under my rib where my daughter often positioned herself, embarrassed to write about everything I'd really seen and experienced since graduating. Two pregnancies, drug dealing, constant arguing, poverty, crack addicts, homelessness. No college or university would want to hear about any of that. Instead it would provide a pretty good reason to deny my application. I needed an accomplishment—just one positive thing. Being employed for several months with the perfume scam was the only thing that came close, and that was a stretch.

This was long before Operation Varsity Blues, a 2019 sting that will lead to fifty people being charged for their involvement in a bribery and cheating scheme to get unqualified teens into elite colleges, revealing just how much power and privilege factor into the college admissions process. For many, the amounts of money and the extent of the fraud will be shocking, but for me, they will only confirm a feeling that was already with me as I sat in front of that computer, pregnant and trying to find a way to convince an institution that I was worthy of admittance.

Like the majority of college applicants, I didn't have a wealthy family behind me to create some story of me being a talented soccer player or to doctor my SAT scores. I hadn't been working with tutors or pricey counselors to ensure admittance into my school of choice, like 26 percent of students who score in the top 70 percent on the SAT.[9] In contrast, I had only met with my guidance counselor a few times during my senior year; other seniors attending high schools that serve predominantly low-income students and students of color often have less than that. Their counselor-to-student ratios are twice the national average—one thousand students per counselor.[10] The words were hard to type as I tried to write the essay, not because I didn't feel capable of going to college as a mother but because I struggled with how to convince others that I was. Years later, in response to the Varsity Blues scandal, Joanne Berger-Sweeney, president of Trinity College, a liberal arts college in Connecticut, will say, "Talent exists across every zip code and every geographic region of the country. Opportunity doesn't always exist across those."

These glaring disparities will be confirmed by the young parents I meet years later, most of whom assumed that they wouldn't go to college because of the significant financial hurdles, little preparation from counselors and teachers, and ultimately an awareness that they didn't fit the mold of what a college student is *supposed* to look like. Naraya, an aspiring teacher who lost both her mother and father by age nineteen, will describe what seems like an impossible path to college. She was held back in the third grade after missing weeks of school to be at the hospital serving as her mother's translator as she battled lupus. These absences, coupled with an undiagnosed learning disorder, made school an intimidating place for her. Naraya couldn't lean on help from her parents because no one in her family had made it past the ninth grade and because, by fifteen, she had lost her mother to the disease.

"All I remember was I hated school growing up," she will tell me. "I felt like I was dumb. I was a slow reader and slow writer. I knew something was wrong with me, but no one got me the help that I needed."

When she became pregnant with her son, Pip, she felt the need to at least try to go to college. "A high school diploma wasn't enough income wise."

Motivated by doing well in a dual-enrollment course at her high school and receiving resources for scholarships from a school-based program for young parents, Naraya enrolled in classes at a community college in Virginia. Still, the hurdles were significant.

"No one in my family went to college," she will tell me. "I had no clue where to start or where to go. All I could think was 'I'm going to do this for Pip.' I don't want him to have a reason to not go to college. I wanted him to see his mom go to college and finish."

After thirty minutes of typing a sentence and then deleting it, I ultimately decided to focus less on what I'd been doing and more on what I *wanted to do*, throwing in the fact that there was a baby and some perfume along the way.

EXPLANATION STATEMENT
The College of William & Mary
Nicole L. Hannans

My whole life, my education was handed to me. For twelve years, I was obligated and expected to go to school, and I made the most of that opportunity. But during the last months of my senior year in high school, the opportunity to continue my education was not as easy to obtain as it had seemed. I had to make a choice between having a child and having an education. Because of my belief in God, I chose to have that child. Many people told me that I was giving up my education and in turn my life, but I never saw it that way. This past year, I have spent most of my time researching and planning how to finance my college career through scholarships and financial aid. I have also contemplated what exactly I want out of the university or college that I plan to attend. In the process, I learned how to live and survive in the real world, and I got a taste of corporate America through an experience with Continental Industries. Now as the 1999 school year approaches, so does that chance to pursue my education that I had always foreseen. Although it will be more difficult this time because I won't have the financial support of my parents, I believe that it will be even more worthwhile because of that fact. I will be able to go to class each day, walk among the grounds of the university, and one day receive my diploma knowing that only I made it possible. It will be an achievement that is solely mine. I have learned through this experience the importance of an education and my desire to pursue it is even stronger. Although it will not be handed to me this time, I can succeed knowing that I have earned it.

I held it in my hands and read it over and over before sealing it inside the envelope addressed to the school's Office of Admissions. Years later, I will try to imagine the conversation about my application around the admissions-panel table. Five or six people reviewing a pile of deferment applications at an institution where most incoming freshmen graduated in the top ten percent of their high school class and came from financially elite families. In 2013, the average family income of William & Mary students will be $270,577, and the median will be $176,400—higher than any other public university.[11] Was it a unanimous decision to admit a pregnant girl with no wealth? Or was there one person fighting for me, refusing to relent until the full panel put their stamp of approval on my application? Did that person who championed for me ever wonder what happened during my time at William & Mary and whether, after everything I was up against, I even graduated?

When my mom got off from work, she drove me to the post office where I mailed off the application, along with an application to Hampton University. Both schools were near the shipyard in Newport News where Rakheim would be working and where he would hopefully find an apartment for us. For now, I completed all of the paperwork without any real, permanent address. I also didn't know if I'd have enough money to even make it through the first semester or if I'd be able to find someone to watch the baby while I went to class. Still, this felt like a major accomplishment. Even if I didn't get into either school or if the stars didn't align perfectly financially and logistically, I had at least taken this first step toward enrolling in college in the fall. We drove back home in silence, preoccupied with the thought that the promise I'd made that day back in Virginia Beach could possibly come to fruition.

· · · · ·

My parents' gray Isuzu traveled back down the long, familiar stretch of I-95. Sitting in the back seat, looking out the window, I found myself on my way to the next place again. They were taking me back to Tidewater, to what I was sure would be the start of my new life with Rakheim and this baby. Despite his infrequent calls and barely mentioning the letters I wrote him regularly, he had proven that he was truly committed to the family we were creating. He had secured a one-bedroom apartment in Newport News right by the shipyard, with the help of the Apprentice School, just like he'd promised. I was meeting him at a Motel 6 in Norfolk where he was renting a room for a couple of weeks until the apartment was ready. I rested my hand against my stomach, which now poked out noticeably underneath my shirt, little white stretch marks beginning to show on my sides. I was excited for him to see how much our baby had grown. I was excited to see *him*. Despite all that I'd learned these past few months about not relying on people and things, I found myself once again anchored to Rakheim and to our new home, so attached that I hinged my whole heart on them.

CHAPTER 8

A SOUL MELTING
ON HOT PAVEMENT

"I DON'T KNOW WHERE I WAS BORN," she will tell me.

I will listen, but it will be hard for me to make sense of those words and hard for me to keep from having an audible, visceral reaction to them.

"I was a crack baby."

She will say all of this without emotion or any acknowledgment of how painful those realities are, as if she's describing someone else's life. Not her own. This is how Alicia, a student in my program who is a mother of two and special-ed teacher working on her bachelor's degree, will talk about her childhood. Her account will come in choppy, dispassionate bursts of information, mirroring her disjointed experiences as a little girl, without a sequence, without order. At the time she will tell me this, her mother will be in the final days of a years-long prison sentence for running an identity-fraud ring.

"I felt like I didn't have my mom or my dad," she will say. "My mom was always on drugs. I was raised by my track coach really. He was like my dad."

One of six children, Alicia will tell me that she thinks she was conceived when her mother was prostituting herself for drugs and money. That's what she's been told, and it's validated by her own painful memory at twelve years old of seeing her mother walk the streets in a fishnet bodysuit. She was seven or eight years old when she met her father, and after that, he came in and out of her life. She will detail a string of moves from apartment to apartment in Northern Virginia, then to a homeless shelter in DC, and then to various people's homes in the Southeast. Despite loving school and being a talented track athlete, by fourteen years old, she was pregnant.

"Don't depend on a man for anything. She taught me that," she will say of her mother. "That's all we heard growing up. Don't give up your power and control."

. . . . .

I sunk into Rakheim's arms, letting them erase me. As soon as my parents left, I clung to him, and cried so hard and long, I had to remind myself to breathe. He kissed my face and grabbed my arms and put his hands all over my belly, almost like he didn't believe I was really there. I ran my finger over his lips and laughed at how silly he looked growing out his dreads again. After the tears and the kisses, I walked around the small dreary room before joining him back on the bed to put my hand against his cheek and tell him how excited I was for the apartment. But a proud man didn't stare back at me. His smile was slowly replaced by a pained look. There was something he didn't want to tell me.

A chill went up my back while he rambled about how he only had enough money for us to stay at the motel for one night, and it would be awhile before we could move into the apartment. So he had arranged for us to stay with the woman, Stacey, who he'd told me about. Stacey, who was addicted to crack. After a few seconds of silence, I stood up and went to the window, pulling aside the heavy flowered curtains. The tears fell quietly while I watched the cold January rain wash over the black pavement in sheets outside and wondered how soon it would turn to ice.

Stacey lived in Indian Lakes, an apartment complex near where my parents used to live. When we pulled up to her building the next morning, I sat in the passenger seat with a sick feeling in my stomach. How was I here, in this situation again? How had I fallen back into this life when for a short time it felt like I'd come so far? I watched as she opened the door and threw her arms around Rakheim. Then she peeked around him and eagerly waved at me, her brown ponytail swinging back and forth behind her.

At first, it was hard to believe Stacey was an addict, but Rakheim said she was one of his biggest customers. When he offered her crack in exchange for letting us stay at her place, she gladly agreed. She was young, pretty, and energetic.

But everything was just beginning to fall apart for Stacey when we moved in. Rakheim told me she'd lost her job at a mortgage company a few weeks before for not showing up for work and missing deadlines. Her wealthy father refused to step in and bail her out of her financial problems this time. Her mother had died in a car accident when Stacey was in the fourth grade. She was married once, but her husband, who introduced her to crack as something to do for an occasional high, left her when she became addicted. She didn't have any friends except for drug dealers and people to get high with. She was happy I was there, offering to make me boxed macaroni and cheese and giving me the plush pink comforter from her bed to ensure I was comfortable at night.

After a while, though, Stacey's addiction was clear. Without a job, she fell behind on rent and couldn't make the payments on her rent-to-own furniture. While she and Rakheim were out selling and scoring crack all day, I was at the apartment, alone, bracing myself for the angry knocks of the various debt collectors. She told me to close all the blinds so no one could see inside. I sat frozen, in the dark, turning down the volume on the TV and waiting for the phone to stop ringing or for the person to walk away from the door. I was never more hungry than when we stayed with Stacey. The kitchen cabinets were always bare because the drugs made her lose her appetite, too. Every few days, I would wait for Rakheim to come home so we could walk to the Farm Fresh behind the apartment complex to at least get some cereal and milk. Honey Bunches of Oats usually served as breakfast, lunch, and dinner. Soon, Stacey was so consumed by her constant need to feel the euphoric numbness, after a while, she stopped buying food for her cats. So Rakheim and I started picking up a few cans of Purina from the store as well.

Stacey was the first White addict I had ever seen, or heard Rakheim talk about. Most of the people he sold to were Black and poor, with few possessions. In contrast, Stacey had a well-off father, a car, her own apartment, a recent career, and closets and dressers full of clothes and shoes. Stacey seemed like a strange, singular case—an outlier—but I would discover that just as there are more White teen mothers than Black and Brown teen mothers in America, there are more White drug users than Black drug users, too. Even when it comes to crack, Stacey's drug and the one that is the main focus of law enforcement, more Whites use it than Blacks. According to the Substance Abuse and Mental Health Services Administration, 5.5 million Whites have used crack during their lifetime, compared to 1.5 million Blacks. Yet, the rate that Blacks are sent to state prison for drug offenses is ten times more than the rate of Whites,[1] and when the average person is asked to picture a drug user, they are more likely to envision Alicia's mother as opposed to someone who looks like Stacey.

The responses to social problems are different when we are led to believe that they are issues that only impact communities of color. There is little incentive to invest in solutions and little empathy for those who are struggling. The opioid epidemic that will come to a peak some twenty years after my time with Stacey will illustrate this. White Americans will account for roughly 80 percent of opioid overdose victims,[2] many living in suburban and rural areas. Blacks will have fewer deaths largely because of the bias in the healthcare system that reduces their access to prescription drugs. In the 1980s, the federal response to curbing the widespread use of crack, particularly in low-income Black communities, was to pass a series of laws with tougher sentencing guidelines. Thirty years later, in response to the opioid epidemic largely affecting Whites, lawmakers from both sides of the aisle will support funding research, rehabilitation, and a push to revise the sentencing guidelines set during the crack era. New York State assemblymember Diana C. Richardson will note this difference during a discussion of the state's response to the opioid epidemic:

> We had a crack cocaine issue in the state of New York, and it impacted communities of color who look like me. We were prosecuted, we were put in jail, children were put in foster care, families were ripped apart. It was treated like a criminal justice issue. Now we have an opioid issue. It is affecting a different demographic, and now it is a health issue, and now we have to put money into diverting individuals from prison into treatment.[3]

• • • • •

I won't meet someone who struggles with opioids until I meet Colleen, a young White mother in our program who was selling and using pain-killers when she conceived her daughter at fourteen years old. The drugs gave her a feeling of control in a chaotic home that was financially stable but emotionally and physically abusive. That chaos began in Indiana when she was placed in foster care at nine months old due to experiencing severe burns and broken bones while in her mother's care. After four years in foster care, followed by four years with her aunt in Pennsylvania, Colleen came back to her mentally unstable mother and stepfather only to endure more abuse that was masked by fancy private schools and a big house. Her boyfriend became her refuge. "Both of us used drugs. I probably used them more regularly because I had access to serious painkillers. I almost overdosed once, and it freaked him out," she will tell me. But it took several failed suicide attempts in Indiana and a move to Virginia before Colleen was finally placed in a safe, loving foster home, just one month before giving birth to her daughter. She will tell me she suspects it's because the Indiana child welfare system was so overwhelmed. I will wonder if the fact that Colleen is White and well-off made her mother's claims that Colleen was schizophrenic and fabricating the abuse more believable. Colleen will mention race when she tells me, almost embarrassed, that the students at her high school called her "Gringa Mama" because "I was the only White girl who was pregnant. All the other pregnant girls were African American or Hispanic. I stuck out."

Teen pregnancy, like drug addiction, has been framed as a social problem only affecting communities of color, with a few outliers of White girls like Colleen who have a child young. This framing means little empathy for young mothers and fathers and scarce investment in diverting them from the welfare system into college—and fulfilling, family-sustaining employment. The way we talk about something, the story we tell ourselves and others—however accurate or inaccurate—has power.

• • • • •

I had gone from finally having the mental space to reapply to college at my parents' house to the chaos of living with a full-blown addict. William & Mary's lush green campus was only an hour away, but it felt completely out of reach, on another planet even. I would need a high-powered rocket ship—or a miracle—to get there.

Sometimes Stacey seemed happy to have us there, cheerily coming through the door with bags of groceries, thanking me for keeping an eye on her cats. Other times, thrown into a rage by Rakheim not having enough crack, she'd run downstairs yelling for us to "Get the fuck out!" only to collapse on the floor minutes later, rubbing her palms against the sides of her face and saying how sorry she was. As each cold, gray day passed, I saw less and less of her bright smile, and her once upbeat laugh was drowned out by constant crying and screaming. When she wasn't in her room smoking, she was gone, looking for more drugs. She was losing weight. Her hair needed to be washed. Dark circles formed around her eyes. She had given up.

Living with a disintegrating addict—and riding around with her while she got high—made me feel like I'd aged far beyond eighteen. During the month we stayed with Stacey, I came to see the world differently, saw its ugliness, and still, it was only a glimpse of what others have endured. Alicia's whole childhood was stolen by the nearly impossible task of surviving her mother's drug addiction. "My mother told me she hated me and wished I would die," she will tell me. "That's something I'll never forget." Joseph, the young father in my program who is now a college graduate, will vividly describe his grandmother walking him through a crack house to buy drugs when he was a young boy, instructing him to keep his eyes on her and to not look back.

One February morning, we left Stacey's apartment. The eviction notice had been tacked on her door for weeks, and we were notified that in days all of her belongings would be emptied out on the sidewalk. We began the familiar ritual of packing our stuff into Tina's Neon, and then, when we were done, we readied ourselves for the usual search for the next place. I sat in the passenger seat and stared at the door of the dark apartment while Rakheim turned the key and started up the car. Even though I would wonder over the years whether Stacey ever got clean and lived a normal life, I never looked back.

• • • • •

My belly was growing round and full of baby. No longer just an idea or something we talked about but couldn't see, she was real. She was a person, stretching and shifting inside a thin cocoon. I felt her movements as faint flutters at first and then as sharp kicks and bursts of energy, especially after I ate a meal or if the music was loud enough. I could lie down on my back and watch my stomach jump. I loved her before, but now watching her taking shape, I adored her.

Somehow through the turmoil at Stacey's, my bladder infection didn't resurface, and I managed to maintain my weight. But a new difficulty emerged. I couldn't get to my doctor appointments. Each time I felt like maybe things were improving, a new challenge reminded me of how bad things still were. After the Cadillac broke down, Rakheim had it towed to a junkyard, where a mechanic gutted it and replaced it with another engine. Despite all of the money Rakheim spent on the repairs, the car broke down again on Virginia Beach Boulevard on our way to one of my checkups. We were stranded on the side of the road, tempted to walk the last few miles. With the Cadillac back in the shop again, and limited access to Tina's Neon, we struggled to make it to the doctor. I will learn that transportation is yet another silent divide between the haves and have-nots. For young parents, it can prevent access to birth control, disrupt prenatal care, or impede well-baby checkups. If you can't find a way to get to these basic things, finding a way to a college campus every day can feel impossible.

Each time we missed an appointment, I worried about the baby and whether we were missing key information or a problem that might snowball into something bigger if it went unchecked. I could hear the receptionist's frustration through the phone as I explained that I hadn't meant to miss the appointment, but we didn't have a way to get there. Asking to reschedule was humiliating. Asking for anything was humiliating. On the day of one of my appointments, Rakheim went to pick up Tina's car but called to tell me he was running late and didn't think he'd make it in time to get me there. He instructed me to call his friend Louis, who went to Tallwood with us and still lived in College Park. Louis said no, the doctor's office was too far. I offered him gas money to which he said, "Man, fuck that. I ain't the baby's father."

When we left Stacey's, I told Rakheim I couldn't sleep on anyone else's floor, so we went back to the Motel 6 in Norfolk, and that's where we stayed for the next two months. Grass was growing through cracks in the parking lot and the sidewalk outside our door, and trash from an overflowing dumpster often washed up alongside the building. Every morning, I passed a few men hanging out of the windows or doors with beer bellies who watched with tired eyes as I walked down to the office and paid for another day's stay. On the way back, I stopped at the vending machine that sat right outside of the office to pick up breakfast—a two-pack of strawberry or brown sugar Pop-Tarts. I woke Rakheim by tickling his ears and nose with the wrapper until he stirred and rose out of bed. Then he'd stand in the doorway, shirtless, and look out at the parking lot, scratching his stomach and back, a cigarette in one hand and his cell phone to his ear. Our time together was always brief. He usually left by 11 a.m., hopping in someone's car, and I would be alone in the room until late at night.

· · · · ·

The day my mother called to tell me I had been accepted to both the College of William & Mary and Hampton University, I was sitting alone in the dimly lit room of a Motel 6, hungry and eight months pregnant. She was calling my name from the receiver that I'd dropped on the floor as I buried my face in my hands, a smile I couldn't control spreading across it. It was as if someone had just opened the door to a high-powered rocket ship and asked me to step inside.

PART TWO

THE URGE TO PUSH

CHAPTER 9

THE STRENGTH IN BETWEEN

THE SHAME I FELT for being a pregnant girl was gone, overcome by other, stronger emotions when they placed my daughter in my arms. I felt no shame for this beautiful life, the tiny, warm weight of her pressed against my chest. I felt no shame for being her mother, in awe of even the single silky black curl from her delicate head that wrapped around my fingertip. I counted her fingers and toes and welcomed each of her tiny breaths against my lips with a grateful heart. In fact, the world and its opinions melted away, leaving just us in that hospital room, wrapped tightly together in a perfect love that made every other emotion I had ever felt seem inferior.

From the moment I saw those two pink lines on the pregnancy test in high school, I fully understood that shame is a strong feeling. Later I would learn that it is also a powerful weapon. When my daughter is fourteen years old, New York officials will use shame in a controversial ad campaign to prevent teens from getting pregnant by showcasing the negative consequences their pregnancies will have on their children's futures. Downtrodden and crying toddlers will appear alongside statements like "I'm twice as likely not to graduate high school because you had me as a teen" and "Think being a teen parent won't cost you?" The campaign will ignite a national debate about the morality and effectiveness of shaming teen parents.

I will be out of town presenting at a conference in Ohio when a reporter calls to ask me to make a statement on the controversy. I won't be able to meet her deadline, but my position on the ads would have been clear. The campaign would have done little to prevent my own teen pregnancy or the majority of the pregnancies I see in my work because they're detached from the realities that most teen pregnancies are unplanned and emerge from chaotic circumstances in which young people feel they have little control or power and few chances of economic mobility. A year before New York City unveils this campaign, researchers will find that poor girls who have babies experience similar economic outcomes in the long term as poor girls who wait to have children.[1] In other words, teen pregnancy doesn't cause poverty, but poverty causes teen pregnancy. Young people at risk of becoming pregnant will look at the ads painting a bleak future with a baby, and they will see a bleak future *with* or *without* a baby. Colleen, who wasn't poor but became pregnant in the midst of physical abuse and opioid use, will reinforce this when she tells me that before her pregnancy, "I didn't care about myself. I thought I was going to die by the age of twenty."

Shame is effective in other ways. Rather than reducing teen pregnancy, shame ironically exacerbates many of the negative outcomes for mother and child that the New York City ads will cite. Worried that she will be judged or mistreated, pregnant girls don't seek crucial prenatal care. Not wanting to be perceived as a failure or as promiscuous, teens hide their pregnancies from people who could potentially help. Feeling like an outcast at school, young mothers stop showing up for class. Shame produces nothing good. It only threatens the health and well-being of both mother and child and hinders opportunities that could improve a mother's ability to provide for her family.

Four years after New York's ad campaign, I will briefly meet the mother of the richest person in the world at an event at the Aspen Institute in DC. As we are finding our seats before the next panel begins, I will muster the courage to hand Jacklyn Bezos my business card and quickly share the work of my organization. As I talk, she will glance up from the card in her hand and say with a grin, "You know, this is my story."

In 1964, barely seventeen years old and a junior in high school, Jacklyn gave birth to Jeff Bezos, who, thirty years later, would start Amazon.

But long before the titan online retail company, administrators at Jacklyn's high school in Albuquerque, New Mexico, tried to prevent her from graduating, telling her she could only come back if she met certain conditions—conditions that were meant to shame her and shield other students from her choices, as if they were contagious. She had to time her arrival and departure so as not to interact with the other students. While in school, she couldn't talk to anyone or eat lunch in the cafeteria. During her graduation, she was forbidden from even walking across the stage with her peers to receive her diploma. She met these conditions, graduated, then started taking night courses while working—even bringing young Jeff and a diaper bag along to class. She finally earned her college degree at the age of forty, just one year after Jeff graduated summa cum laude from Princeton University in 1986, with a degree in computer science and electrical engineering.

It's an interesting exercise trying to imagine how different Jacklyn and Jeff's lives would be had she not met those conditions. And how different *our lives* would be. Today, we associate the Bezos name with success, prosperity, and progress, but fifty years ago, Jacklyn was just a teen mom, unworthy of a seat in the cafeteria, and Jeff was just her baby. It's tempting to think that because we no longer have to talk in whispers about teen pregnancy and because shows like MTV's *Teen Mom* have put the topic on major platforms, shame is a thing of the past, but from the moment I disclosed my pregnancy, people tried to impose it on me, and I won't meet another teen mother who hasn't been shamed—no matter how recently she had her baby.

In 2017, after being named National Teacher of the Year by President Barack Obama but before becoming a congresswoman in the US House of Representatives, Jahana Hayes will stand on stage in front of the six hundred people at our annual fundraising event to tell her story. She will frequently pause, looking down at her hands on the podium, only to be encouraged to continue by the crowd's applause. She will admit, through tears, that her emotion comes from the fact that it is the first speaking engagement where she has been asked to tell her story of becoming pregnant at sixteen. Shame is a silencer.

· · · · ·

The doctor scheduled my induction for 9:30 a.m. on Thursday, May 20, 1999, ten days after my due date. The idea of scheduling birth was strange to me. I pictured every child coming into the world spontaneously, starting with a startled woman looking down at a puddle of her water on the floor, which would then incite a frenzy of grabbing the diaper bag and car keys and embarking on a scary ride to the hospital—possibly with a police escort. For the past ten months, I had envisioned my birth going this way, but when my due date came and went, the doctor started preparing me for the possibility of inducing labor. The longer my baby stayed in my belly, the higher the risk of complications.

Like many young mothers, I hadn't taken a childbirth or Lamaze class. Most of what I knew about giving birth I'd gotten from a used copy of *What to Expect When You're Expecting* and a few conversations with a friend's younger sister, who had a premature, three-pound baby the month before. Many nights, I fell asleep with the book in my hands, only skimming the chapter the next morning before heading down to the motel office to pay for another day's stay. I could tell you the fruit equivalent of my baby each month—a cabbage, a pineapple, a cantaloupe, and eventually a watermelon—but I couldn't tell you what was about to happen to me, to my body. Aside from certain pain—the aches and helplessness of my miscarriage were still fresh in my memory—the rest was a mystery. For me, anticipating childbirth was like standing on train tracks, feeling the steel vibrate under my feet, hearing the horn of the approaching train, and being unable to move.

If there was ever a time when I needed my mother, it was now. Just as she had held my hand through each of my asthma attacks, gasping to get enough air in my lungs, I needed her to hold my hand through this. Over the past several months, we talked on the phone regularly, the promise of a little person, who would soon need both of us, seemed to bring us closer. I had questions about how to smooth away my stretch marks and why I was craving cornstarch. She had advice for my achy back and a list of questions I should ask the doctor during my visits. We laughed about silly things, and when we hung up, I'm sure she cried about the big things.

I didn't have a birth plan. At nineteen, the idea that I could have any control over what happened in the labor and delivery room never even occurred to me. My doctor, the same doctor who neglected to tell me about the need for backup contraception during my first week on the pill, didn't inform me that I could decide against pain medication during labor or opt for a different position other than laying on my back while I delivered my baby. My mother wasn't all that aware of birth plans either since women didn't begin documenting these preferences with their healthcare providers until the early 1980s, after she gave birth to me. Like the women before her, and like most young mothers, she had little say in how she brought Anika and me into the world.

My student Naraya was nineteen, like me, when she gave birth to her son, Pip, and she will describe it as a near-death, traumatizing experience that no one ever fully explained. After laboring for more than twenty-four hours with no dilation and excruciating pain, she was whirled into a large white operating room and prepped for a cesarean. She remembers looking at her husband under the bright lights as she went under anesthesia and telling the nurses and doctor that she couldn't breathe. They responded by saying that everything was fine and busily moved around the room, preparing for the surgery. Then her hand went limp in her husband's hand, and her eyes rolled back in her head. Her husband told her this was when they forced him out of the room to perform CPR.

"I woke up in ICU," she will say. "I didn't get to give Pip his first bottle or diaper change. The first time I saw my baby was on my husband's phone."

Naraya tried to ask questions, but the nurses and doctors seemed to brush her off, telling her to focus on her new baby instead. At home, she researched what could have gone wrong, and found that they likely made a mistake when they gave her the epidural, putting it too high in her back and "cutting off my airway." Her obstetrician passed away six years after Pip was born, and when Naraya picked up her chart from his office, she saw the delivery notes for the first time. She couldn't understand all of them, but she discerned a note about how rare the complication was, "like being struck by lightning twice."

"They didn't give me the right answers," she will say. "They kept trying to cover it up. They knew how to work me because I was young."

. . . . .

I waved off the epidural. While the pain was almost intolerable, I knew it was time. I didn't have to know all of the terms or the purpose of each piece of equipment to feel nature was taking over and making its own decisions. With the next grueling wave, my back instinctually straightened, and my body readied itself to push. When I will reach this peak in labor bringing my other three children into the world, the midwives will calmly tell me to listen to my body and push if I need to, but when the nurse summoned this doctor, he came into the room shaking his head, no. He stood at the foot of the bed and told me it was too soon to push. But God and babies work on their own time, and Nerissa Glori was born at 5:19 p.m., after five minutes of pushing so hard that all of the blood vessels in my face popped. Warm, purple, and slippery, they placed her on my chest. Eight pounds, nine ounces, and twenty and a half inches. I laughed in disbelief and exhaustion while my mom smoothed back the curls that clung to my forehead and with tears in her eyes told me that Nerissa looked like me and Anika when we were born. Standing on the other side of the bed, Rakheim hovered over us, proud and speechless.

• • • • •

Two months before Nerissa was born and just a few weeks shy of Rakheim's first day at the shipyard, we pulled out of the Motel 6 parking lot for the last time and headed to a one-bedroom apartment on Thirty-First Street in downtown Newport News. St. James Terrace was a small collection of red brick buildings constructed in the 1930s. The apartments sat on a hill, overlooking the James River, in the middle of decaying downtown buildings, coal factories, and low-income housing. East End, an almost exclusively Black neighborhood riddled with crime and neglected public housing, was just blocks away. While we were moving in, one of the area's success stories had just moved out of East End where he was born and raised. Michael Vick, a child of teen parents and a future NFL star, was in his first year at Virginia Tech on a football scholarship. He will say in an interview three years later, "Sometimes, I would go fishing even if the fish weren't biting, just to get out of there."[2] From our window, the massive naval ships that Rakheim would soon be building and repairing sat docked along that same river. I could almost taste the musky water as I dragged loads of clothes to the laundry room in another building. Sailors coming on and off the ship would whistle and wave.

Everything about the apartment was modest, but finally, after more than a year of sleeping on couches and floors, staring at other people's walls, bracing myself for their looks of sympathy or irritation when we asked for a place to stay, we had a small place in the world.

In my mind, the root of our unhappiness was our precarious housing situation. Not having a place to call our own was humiliating and taxing, and those feelings were exacerbated by the fact that we had a baby on the way. Our homelessness ate away at happy moments and darkened bright spots. I couldn't respect Rakheim against the backdrop of a seedy, dirty motel and on a daily diet of stale Pop-Tarts. At the time, this tension felt uniquely ours, like yet another failure all our own, but in 2015, the Institute for Children, Poverty & Homelessness will find that "homeless mothers are more likely than housed mothers to experience domestic violence, mental illness, and substance abuse." It turns out, we were just one of many wandering families living in turmoil.

Our apartment should have been the antidote then—four walls and a roof to remedy all of our problems. The first week at St. James made me feel like it might actually be the fix I'd been waiting for. Rakheim and I spent our days putting dishes on the shelves and squeezing furniture through the slender front door, and our nights lounging on the bed, his hand resting on my belly in the evening light. But the excitement of something shiny and new just masked our underlying issues and frustrations, and it wore off quickly.

Our first fight in the apartment raged on for hours, full of pent-up anger and resentment, rushing right back at us with a vengeance. When it finally died down, we collapsed on opposite sides of the bed. A few minutes passed before he stood up and strained to open the old, stubborn window. I watched him pull a box of Newports out of his back pocket, snap the container against the palm of his hand, and light a cigarette. Then he blew one long cloud of smoke out through the screen. I told him he wasn't supposed to smoke around me. He stared straight ahead, silent.

"I hate you sometimes," I said. "I really do."

"I hate you too," he said.

· · · · ·

A part of me always knew that I'd be parenting alone, but I was holding on to the slim chance that Rakheim could change. From the start of our relationship, he was there without really being *there*, and while bringing a life into the world had changed me, it hadn't changed him. He loved Nerissa. I could see that in his eyes while he looked down at her in the delivery room. But he wasn't fully present, and maybe, looking back, he didn't know how to be. I didn't understand it. I didn't understand his constant need to disappear. Not long after they moved us into a room in the maternity ward, he made up an excuse about needing to pick up a friend, and he was gone. He didn't wander back into the room until sometime in the early morning hours and slept most of the next day before holding her for a few minutes and leaving again.

That first night, it was my mom who slept curled up in the chair by my bed, and together, we woke up to rock and hold Nerissa each time she cried while marveling at her little stretches and coos. When she was hungry, my mom helped me get her to latch on so I could breastfeed, something she had done with both Anika and me. Each time I had to get up and go to the bathroom, my mom propped me up as I shakily put one foot in front of the other to get to the toilet. She did what so many mothers of young mothers do—stepped in to fill the shoes of a partner who isn't there or who isn't there enough.

When a young mother talks about how hard the first few weeks at home with her baby were, most people won't fully understand. They will compare it to the sleep-deprived, excruciatingly painful recovery that most women experience. But while older mothers may have the benefit of a partner or a strong social network to help through the newborn phase, young mothers often find themselves alone, isolated, navigating uncharted waters, and dealing with the many stressors that were there before the baby—unstable housing, domestic violence, no money for formula or diapers. Chelsea will tell me how much she struggled after her grandmother, who had come from Trinidad to help her with Ava, left: "When she left, I was exhausted. It took me a while to get back on my feet after that. It was the hardest thing to get my body back up and moving." Ana, who brought her son home to an empty house because her mother was always working and her son's father wanted nothing to do with them, will say she cried so much in those first few months: "Part of my tears were like, why did I let myself get into this situation? I had a lot of anger and sadness about raising a child." For young mothers, this can be the hardest time in a never-ending string of hard times, when you're trying to make the impossible, possible, caring for a brand-new life with such little physical strength of your own.

My mother stayed for a week, cooking meals, buying supplies, and trying to sleep on the stiff Goodwill couch between Nerissa's late-night feedings and Rakheim drifting in drunk or high at 2 a.m. or 3 a.m. Even with her help, I struggled. I was recovering from a third-degree tear, which meant I was still bleeding heavily, and just getting up from a seated position took every bit of my strength. My milk came in on the second day home, and I was too engorged for Nerissa to latch on. She screamed endlessly until I was able to manually express a small amount of milk for her to drink. My mom rushed to the store and bought an electric pump, which allowed me to fill a whole bottle. When the engorgement went down a bit, and Nerissa finally nursed, it was as if every drop of my energy went right into her milk. Sometimes by the end of a feeding, we'd both fall asleep, and my mother would quietly gather her up and hold her while I slept.

The day my mother left, I stood on the sidewalk long after she had climbed into her car and drove out of sight, and I sobbed. Raw with both grief and giving life, I unraveled there in the warmth of the May sun until, attempting to pull myself together, I finally began making the slow and painful journey back up the stairs to the apartment, where Nerissa and Rakheim were waiting. Just before I reached the door to our building, I stopped, feeling the gaze of the cathedral-like warships that sat against the backdrop of the perfect baby-blue sky and the river's sparkling waves, and turned to look at them. They stood, unyielding, armed, and resolute.

· · · · ·

College was always the goal. Thanks to my parents, it had been the goal my entire life. Help with homework, trips to the library, consequences for anything below a C on my report card, staying up late to finish the volcano for the science fair, moving to certain neighborhoods for the right schools, paying for my AP exams and my SATs. Each of these acts prepared and positioned me for college as the guaranteed, next step after high school. When I discovered my pregnancy, it became a more important goal. College morphed from a leisurely, existential exploration of who I was and who I wanted to be into a very practical means to an end. I understood how slim the prospects of adequately providing for a child—even simple things like a place to live and a working car—were without a postsecondary credential. Now that Nerissa was here, college had transformed yet again into an urgent, nonnegotiable imperative. Like every young parent I will meet over the years, I wanted my child to have the world, and college felt like the best way to place it in her hands.

With two acceptance letters in front of me, I decided to go to William & Mary. My dad said it was one of only eight schools in the nation called a "Public Ivy," where you could receive a superior education without paying top dollar in tuition. The prestige, he said, would open doors like it had done for Anika, who was now finishing her graduate degree at Yale. I wanted those open doors, those opportunities, but I worried that that same prestige might also make it hard for me to ever reap those benefits. William & Mary was the perfect place for people like Anika, who effortlessly graduated in the top 10 percent of their high school class, but not for me, who did well in school but never had a chance at valedictorian, and certainly not for someone who had a baby. Going to college would make little difference in my life if I went there and dropped out. Even as I made preparations to start there in the fall, I couldn't shake the nagging feeling that I wouldn't be able to handle it.

When the bill came for the three-hundred-dollar deposit needed to start my enrollment process, Rakheim put a stack of cash in my hand and smiled. The next day, I bought a money order from the 7-Eleven near St. James and mailed it off in a green envelope, along with a signed commitment card. But I would need more than three hundred dollars to go to college, and the plan for paying for my first semester was shaky. When the enrollment process began, I hadn't given birth to Nerissa yet, which meant I was still considered a dependent, even though I had been on my own for more than a year. As a dependent, I would have my parents' income considered in my financial aid award, preventing me from receiving enough money to pay my tuition.

I had been assigned a financial aid officer, a young Black woman named Mrs. Currie, who later insisted that I call her Tammy. After a couple of phone calls, she told me that once I had Nerissa, I could submit a copy of her birth certificate to the financial aid office, and they would reprocess my award. This plan made me nervous. I was signing on the dotted line, relying on a calculation that would require everything to align perfectly. What if there was a delay in getting the baby's birth certificate? What if I was able to get a copy of the birth certificate, but it was lost in the mail? What if they received it at the financial aid office, but someone forgot to put it in my file? What if I didn't give birth on my due date, causing me to miss the deadline to change my dependent status? These weren't irrational fears. Years later, my staff and I will become so accustomed to helping young parents maneuver out of endless loops of paperwork mishaps at their colleges and at social service offices that we will only share the most extreme stories.

I carried these what-ifs around in my head every day, trying to anticipate and solve for every possible schism in the plan. I did this while attempting to survive life in a Motel 6, living with the stress of a toxic relationship, and growing a baby. I was hoping for a lifeline as I worked through the equation, some sort of assurance. During a visit to my parents' house Easter weekend, with the paperwork spread out on their kitchen table, I asked if they'd be willing to take out a small PLUS loan, a federal loan that parents of dependent students can use to assist with college costs, just for $2,500, to ensure that I could at least register for classes while the paperwork was ironed out.

"No," my dad said quickly and sternly, as if he and my mom had talked this through before. "We're not gonna do that. We're not taking out any loans. You want to do this, you do it yourself." Then he refilled his drink and went back downstairs to his music.

Before my mom could say anything, I quickly gathered up the papers and left the room. Upstairs on the futon, I hugged my belly and cried.

• • • • •

Now, with Nerissa here, I found myself in a strange limbo, somewhere between dependent and independent, between an incoming college freshman and a lost teen mother, between being worthy of a public ivy and undeserving of a seat in the cafeteria. Only two things felt sure and certain. One, I was Nerissa's mother. And two, what she needed from me then, and what she would need from me always, was my strength. Not my shame.

CHAPTER 10

ALL GOOD THINGS

MY FEET DIDN'T BELONG on the 1,200-acre, perfectly manicured campus. They awkwardly shuffled from building to building under the towering trees in cheap black Walmart flip-flops while patches of sunlight danced over them. Other students casually strolled along the winding brick paths, sipping from expensive water bottles and Starbucks cups full of iced coffee, or lounged on their backs in the luxuriant green grass of the Sunken Garden in the middle of Old Campus. Some families lingered for long goodbyes or to empty the last crate of towels from the trunk of their double-parked cars.

Today was orientation. I crowded into William & Mary Hall, a 24,000-square-foot facility that housed basketball games and other big events, along with hundreds of other freshmen to be officially welcomed to the school and receive pertinent information for ensuring that my semester started smoothly. The school's colors—green and gold—decorated the walls and seats. A flag hung high above us that read "Tribe Pride." I'd been to William & Mary Hall twice before—once when I was fourteen years old for a big concert with Anika and then a couple of years later for her three-hour graduation ceremony, during which President George H. W. Bush, the commencement speaker, called the school "a place of possibilities."

With goody bags full of school-branded swag at our feet, we took the honor pledge and listened to various students and President Sullivan talk about what a great four years it was going to be. To point out how accomplished our incoming class was, the president asked all of the students who had earned the distinction of either valedictorians and salutatorians of their high school senior class to stand, and it seemed as if the entire crowd rose from their seats. The welcome speeches echoed through the stadium while I glanced at the faces of the other freshmen around me, some eager, some completely uninterested, very few the color of mine. I hung on every word, trying to commit each piece of advice to memory, mostly because I couldn't believe I'd made it this far, and I was scared that if I missed even one thing, I wouldn't make it any further. I knew that I was a glaring irregularity in a sea of White faces, exacerbating the feeling that my being there was a mistake.

Those of us who have felt othered in some way are often the first to recognize how deficient our systems are. Fifty years earlier, President Harry Truman's Commission on Higher Education elevated the reasons so many students are left out of postsecondary opportunities: "For the great majority of our boys and girls, the kind and amount of education they may hope to attain depends, not on their own abilities, but on the family or community into which they happened to be born or, worse still, on the color of their skin or the religion of their parents."[1] President Truman is the only US president in the twentieth century who did not graduate from college, because his parents couldn't afford it. In 1948, William & Mary presented him with an honorary degree, one of twenty-two he received over his lifetime.

As tempting as it was, I couldn't be swept up in the green and gold excitement of the day, couldn't forget that I wasn't like all of them. I was different, and my situation left little room for error. I was a full-time student, taking thirteen credits, with a nearly three-month-old baby. I'd be in class all day on Mondays, Wednesdays, and Fridays while Paula graciously agreed to watch Nerissa. This meant daycare was free, but it also meant leaving Newport News at 7 a.m. with all of Nerissa's supplies for the day, including carefully sealed bags of my breast milk, to drop Rakheim off at work and drive south to Paula's house in Portsmouth, then driving back up north again through Newport News to arrive on campus in Williamsburg right before my first class started. At 5 p.m., at the end of my last class, I rushed back across campus to the car to do it all over again, finally arriving home with a tired, cranky baby at 7 p.m. The whole trip totaled three and a half hours and 150 miles. Two decades later, the College Board will find that transportation costs for an average postsecondary commuter student accounts for 17 percent of their living expenses. My organization's own research will reveal that more than 20 percent of college students with children cite transportation as one of their most significant challenges to finishing school.[2] Each day, the fact that I had made it to campus and back home felt like a miracle—one that I wasn't sure I could pull off again.

Being able to pay for my first semester was a similarly uneasy feeling. I quickly obtained Nerissa's birth certificate, as well as a second copy to mail to the financial aid office, and prayed that all of the what-ifs fell together in time for the fall semester. Tammy Currie called to confirm that she had received the birth certificate and promptly processed my appeal, just like she'd promised. By July, I qualified as an independent student and was able to take out $8,500 in loans to pay for my tuition, books, and a computer to work on at home since I wouldn't be able to use any of the computer labs on campus. I underestimated how much books would cost, how expensive meals on campus would be, and how much gas the Cadillac would guzzle driving 150 miles three days a week. These miscalculations meant I didn't always have the books I needed for class or food to eat during the day. I was starting my first semester already behind.

Nerissa was still tiny, nursing, and not sleeping through the night, and I was still trying to figure out the rhythm of motherhood. My plan was to do all of my studying on Tuesdays and Thursdays when we were at home together, but when she wasn't sleeping, she required my full attention for feedings every few hours, playtime, and soothing her cries. This relegated most of my work to nights, interfering with my sleep and pumping schedule. At school, there were no lactation rooms so I pumped in the bathroom stalls in between classes while other students curiously peeked through the cracks in the door, trying to figure out what was causing the buzzing syphoning sound. At home, I pumped again after putting Nerissa to bed then positioned myself in front of my computer to plow through as much studying as I could, sometimes until early morning. A tall stack of books, mostly novels for my English classes, sat beside me on the fifty-dollar self-assembled desk as I worked, constantly reminding me of how much reading I still had to do.

Even without working a full- or part-time job on top of going to college, like 90 percent of my future students and 70 percent of all college students,[3] I was feeling the effects of "time poverty," something that researchers at the City University of New York's Office of Institutional Research and Assessment will cite in 2018 as being one of the most arduous challenges for college students with children. They will find that parenting students have approximately 50 percent less available time for coursework than their non-parenting peers, yet they face the same academic expectations. This meant I was attending one of the top public universities in the country with only half the time other students had to get all of my work done, and the expectation at William & Mary was not just to get it done but to get it done *well*.

I emerged from the stadium, squinting in the late afternoon sun, and made my way toward Rakheim's Cadillac, which stuck out like a long silver boat in the parking lot. People brushed past me in all directions, following their orientation advisors to the various cafeterias on campus for dinner while chatting about the first parties of the year and which sorority or fraternity to join. That morning, I had been erroneously folded into a group of transfer students because of my rare off-campus status as a first-time freshman, and my orientation advisor had wandered off with another group, not sure what to do with me exactly. I didn't tell her, or anyone else in the group, that I was a mother, sensing that it would have caused even more confusion and frigidity. For the rest of the day, I roamed the campus by myself, armed only with the orientation agenda and a map. Now, in the crowd, I didn't see my advisor or any of the transfer students. It didn't matter. Even if I'd had a meal plan, I wouldn't have been able to join them. It was 6:30 p.m., past the time to make the nearly two-hour drive to Portsmouth to pick up Nerissa. My breasts were achy and full of milk, and I needed to figure out what to cook for dinner. When I reached the Cadillac, I shot a brief glance back at the campus—each large building like a giant mountain to be scaled—while my heart whispered, "Thank you."

• • • • •

Like so many students who don't fit the narrow definition of "college student," each day, at school, I put on a brilliant performance, working hard to fit in, to mask my differences. At home, I also performed, pretending to be content. A quiet brainiac, completely submerged in the content of each of my classes—so much so that I didn't have time for making friends or anything else. And also a happy new mother, easily keeping all of the many balls in the air, unphased by the chaos of our home.

For anyone taking a quick, surface look at my situation, the stage was set. Nerissa was growing into a plump, happy baby. I'd started my freshman year of college just as I'd promised my mother the day she found out about my pregnancy. Rakheim and I had moved into a larger, two level, two-bedroom apartment on Jefferson Avenue, about ten minutes away from St. James. He was still playing football for the Apprentice School and working at the shipyard. I was able to buy my own car so I wouldn't have to drop Rakheim off at work and pick him up on my way to and from school. It had all of the appearances of progress and pieces falling into place, but in reality, everything was coming apart at the seams.

Rakheim was like a ghost in the house, coming home only to sleep and eat, in between working, football, and selling. We didn't share the responsibility of waking up with Nerissa at night or give each other breaks when one of us was pushed to the brink with exhaustion. A quick kiss on her forehead on his way in or out of the apartment comprised most of Rakheim's interactions with Nerissa. I took her to all of her doctor appointments, and when she was hospitalized for a virus at six weeks old, he was again absent. I sat alone in the emergency room, helpless, as doctors conducted blood tests and performed a spinal tap, and once she was admitted, I sat alone praying by her bed, which was surrounded by a plastic protective covering. I lived in the same home as my daughter's father, but I was raising her almost entirely on my own.

I was always on duty. Taking a shower was a luxury, and I rarely had moments to myself for relaxing or refueling. Any free time was swallowed up by her feedings and diaper changes and fits of crying. I couldn't watch TV or take a nap. I was so stressed and consumed with caring for her that I would forget to eat and realized one night when I was doubled over in pain that I hadn't urinated in a week. My student Nija will describe a similar lonely existence living in the same house as her boyfriend in the months that followed the birth of their son: "It was terrible. I went through postpartum depression. I felt like I didn't want to live anymore. I was obligated to be there at home with the baby all the time. It was never about me anymore."

Rakheim and I didn't leave St. James simply because we wanted an upgrade. We were forced to leave because the property wouldn't allow three people in a one-bedroom unit. We found the new apartment on Jefferson Avenue in South Newport News a few weeks after Nerissa was born despite Rakheim complaining about paying seventy-five dollars more each month in rent. I was excited about having more space and making the second bedroom into Nerissa's nursery. Rakheim soon became excited, too, when he realized that the new place sat across the street from an outdated, run-down hotel called King's Arms that thrived as a hot spot for drugs. Dealers would rent out a room for a couple of days and set up shop for addicts to come through and spend all of their money or trade in cars, TV's, camcorders, and jewelry for drugs. Rakheim would become one of them, eventually spending more time at King's Arms than at work or playing football.

We bought another car because the Cadillac broke down again, and we were worried about me not having reliable transportation to get to campus. It was a white 1992 Subaru station wagon from a tiny dealership on Jefferson Avenue. We used seven hundred dollars from my loan money as a down payment, and after that, we'd pay one hundred dollars a month without interest. The car was supposed to be mine, but if Rakheim was at the apartment when I came home from school, he would grab the keys and leave.

I chose my battles carefully, knowing that each time I challenged Rakheim, it could result in a horrible fight, and sometimes he'd take his frustrations out on Nerissa, yelling for her to shut up when she cried. Since having Nerissa and the start of the semester, our arguments were becoming more intense and whenever I alluded to leaving or ending the relationship, he said or did something crazy. Once, while arguing in the car on our way home from Paula's house, I told him I couldn't take it anymore, and he threatened to run the station wagon off the road and kill all three of us. Another time, he threw Nerissa's bowl of cereal across the room while she sat in her high chair screaming and told me I'd never be able to survive without him. After every argument, I'd pull her close to me and wipe away both of our tears, trying to force a smile the same way my mother used to, assuring her that Mommy was okay. But I wasn't okay, and she wouldn't stop crying until I did.

I'd been riding this roller coaster with Rakheim for a long time, but something was changing inside of me. I wasn't exactly sure if it was motherhood or being able to sit in a classroom again or a combination of both, but I was beginning to see Rakheim and our crazy lifestyle differently. When I looked into Nerissa's eyes, I wanted more.

It took one violent Friday night to wholly convince me that I was done with Rakheim. The fight began in our living room after I'd put Nerissa to bed and sat at the desk, working on a paper. He didn't want to pay the rent that month, insisting that he instead needed the money for a sound-system upgrade in the Cadillac, which was working again. It was normal for him to pressure me to pay bills late or not at all, but this time, I refused, and my defiance set him on fire. He loomed over me, his blaring voice too big for the room. When I couldn't take it anymore, I shot up from the chair and yelled back, meeting his eyes as they warned me to sit. He pressed his nose against mine and called me a "fucking bitch." I pushed him and tried to run upstairs, but his arms yanked me back, and we stumbled into the dining room where he wrestled me down to the floor, sat on top of me, and pinned my arms down under his knees.

Tears streamed down my temples while I screamed in pain, begging for him to get off, but I could tell by the look in his eyes that he didn't really see *me* anymore. With a stinging grip on my wrist, he snatched my arm free from under the weight of his leg, jerked it in the air, then forcefully snapped it down, using my hand to slap me hard across my face. The burn was only interrupted by a second strike against my cheek and then the feeling of his spit on my face. As he pushed himself off of me, I curled myself together. Then he stood up and stormed out of the apartment.

With my head ringing, I sat up slowly. My skin was warm and throbbing against my hand. The bridge of my nose and my cheekbone felt raw. Even my gums hurt. I finally stood, went to the door of the apartment, and locked it before sitting on the couch, my back upright and my eyes staring straight ahead. The world seemed so small, like everything revolved around this tiny living room where my universe had been torn apart. I relived the fight in my head, seeing his face above me, haunted by its unfamiliarity.

About twenty minutes later, he was back at the door, trying to open it, banging and yelling my name. I told him I wasn't letting him in, and I wanted him to leave us alone, but before I could finish my sentence, the door burst open, the molding and lock splintering off in little pieces all around the room. He sprinted past me, possessed, shouting threats as he rushed upstairs and came down with Nerissa in his arms, holding her almost like a football. She was disoriented and starting to cry, wearing just the onesie I had put her to bed in. I grabbed at his coat, frantically asking him what he was doing while he put her in the stroller that rested against the wall and pushed me away. Then he walked outside, and together, they were swallowed up by the dark, cool October night.

After fifteen grueling minutes deliberating whether I should call the police, he came back. In silence, I took her out of the stroller and rushed upstairs to her bedroom, where I thanked God for answering my prayer and remembered my promise that I'd find the strength to leave Rakheim if he brought her home safely to me.

At the time, I didn't fully understand what happened, and over the years, it will still be hard for me to name it. My understanding of domestic violence was shaped and formed in high school by photos of Nicole Brown Simpson's purpled eyes and scratched face scrolling across the TV screen during O.J. Simpson's trial. Even when I'm older, I will not see myself in Yvette Cade, a woman who will be set on fire by her ex-husband in 2005 at the cell phone store where she worked, leaving her with burns all over her head and upper body. I had no bruises, no black eyes, no burns. I had aches and pains and regrets, wishing I hadn't yelled and said things that likely helped to escalate our exchanges. My own struggle with the toxicity of this relationship will help me understand the many young mothers in my program who will have a hard time identifying when their partners cross the line and what constitutes abuse, some who *will* have broken bones and black eyes. Some for whom the answer should be obvious.

Rakheim crawled into the bed sometime in the middle of the night and cried so hard the bed shook. He promised me he would never put his hands on me again. I lay on my side staring into the darkness, feeling nothing in my heart for him. For the next few days, we moved around the apartment in silence. I dropped him off at work and watched him walk toward the shipyard in the early morning light holding his lunch box and carrying his hard hat, his head hung low. In the evening, he washed the dishes and fed Nerissa in an effort to show me how sorry he was. Eventually, we started laughing again, but the damage had been done. It was like watching someone from the window of a train falling farther and farther back in the distance.

No one at William & Mary knew that any of these things were happening in my life. Few people even knew that I was a mother. My advisor was an art professor whose office was located in the art complex, on the opposite side of campus from where most of my classes were held. During our first meeting at the start of my first semester, I found him sketching in his classroom, annoyed by having to be pulled away from his work for our appointment. The only thing that sparked his interest was me mentioning Anika, who happened to be his student during her days as an art and economics major at William & Mary. Our conversation revealed how little he knew about the English Department, which wasn't helpful because I wanted to be an English major, and how little he cared about anything outside of his discipline. A couple of days before our second meeting, he canceled due to an emergency and never responded to my requests to reschedule.

In 2003, the year I will graduate from college, US universities will average one advisor for every 282 students.[4] Fifteen years later, when I am working with young parents in college and when Nerissa is a college student herself, the ratio will be one advisor for every 375 students. The ratio at community colleges will be even worse: typically one advisor for every 1,000 students, and in some financially strapped institutions, it will be as high as one to 1,700. Most students won't earn a degree within two or four years due to a myriad of challenges, but strong academic counseling could serve as a lifeline, providing critical information, connections to resources, and emotional support, which might accelerate how quickly they are able to earn their credential. My program will compensate for this deficiency, serving as academic advisors and life coaches to hundreds of teen parents working toward their degrees. But there will be too many students who will fall through the cracks without this type of support. More than half of students who are parenting—students like me—leave college without earning their degree.[5]

Soon I felt more comfortable on campus than I did at home with Rakheim. I loved the energy of William & Mary, abuzz with curiosity and learning and new ideas as people flowed from building to building and class to class. I moved along with them, carrying an official school ID in my wallet and a black over-the-shoulder bag that Anika had given me from her days in college, weighed down by my books. I etched out a solid pumping schedule and identified a favorite bathroom in Tucker, the English building, where I liked to pump my milk. I eagerly sat in the front row of each of my classes, hoping to absorb as much information as I could because I knew how limited my time was at home.

Through the chaos, I managed to finish my first semester with two B+'s and two B's and called my mom as soon as the grades were posted.

• • • • •

January marked the start of the second semester. By January, Rakheim had been fired. He'd stopped showing up for work, and he'd quit the football team. After studying all day upstairs in the bed with Nerissa while she slept and rolled around in the blankets and cuddled with me, I would walk downstairs on a Saturday night to find him and his friends counting thousands of dollars in stacks on our living room floor, laughing and joking while their guns were lying on the dining room table. Occasionally, there would be faint knocks at the door from people wanting to buy drugs, unable to wait for Rakheim to set up shop at King's Arms across the street.

Things seemed to be spiraling further and further out of control. I didn't know where he was for days. No calls, no word about whether he was even alive. Once he and his friends were arrested for robbing vending machines, and I wouldn't find out until Tina posted his bail. Another time, during a snowstorm that shut down the roads, he showed up in the middle of the night insisting that we drive to a hotel in Virginia Beach to stay for a few days because the police raided King's Arms, and he was worried they'd come to our apartment looking for him. Sometimes I slept on the couch because I couldn't stand the thought of him touching me. If I took Nerissa with me to visit my parents for a weekend, I would come home and find condoms in the trash can, and sometimes I overheard him on the phone with other women when he thought I was asleep.

• • • • •

After three and a half years, a baby, and everything we had been through, I was finally determined to leave Rakheim. For months, I'd been skillfully crafting an extraction plan. I made so many visits to Tammy's office that the receptionist just told me to go right in each time I walked through the door. Tammy helped me review my loans and grants and find any extra money. She said it would be a struggle, but I *could* survive on my own. She put me in contact with the school's Residence Life office, and I applied for a family-housing apartment on campus. The rent would be $480 per month, and if I got it, it would be available in August. I focused all of my attention on how to convince Rakheim that me moving to Williamsburg would be the best thing for us. I couldn't tell him outright that I was leaving him, so instead, I encouraged him to apply to Norfolk State University, about an hour away from William & Mary, where he could possibly play football and earn a degree. If both of us went to college, I said, we could give Nerissa a better life. As a football player, he'd have to live on campus, so Nerissa and I would need our own place to stay. I could find us something in Williamsburg, and when both of us were done with school, we could all live together again.

No matter how right the decision is, a woman still feels guilty for tearing her family apart. Rakheim didn't make it any easier for me. So many nights, we lay in bed talking about it until early morning, his eyes full of so much pain and confusion. I would convince him—most of the time through tears—that everything would be okay, and when I was alone, I'd try to convince myself of the same thing.

One hazy day in August, I left Rakheim. I packed up a U-Haul truck with all of my stuff, leaving the apartment empty and hollow, except for the few things he planned to keep—the couch, a TV he'd gotten from an addict, and trash bags full of his clothes. It was time to go. I did one last sweep of the second floor and found one of Nerissa's pink sneakers on its side at the bottom of the closet in our bedroom. I held it in my hand as I stopped to look out of the window at the truck waiting in the parking lot below and the long stretch of Jefferson Avenue beyond. Then, I walked down the stairs, each of my steps on the dusty hardwood floors echoed through the apartment and reminded me that there was nothing left.

CHAPTER 11

FREEDOM DANCE

PARALLEL, FACING FRONT, my bare feet grounded themselves on the cool "marley" floor of the dance studio. My spine curved over, knees slightly bent, and arms hung comfortably at my sides as I waited. I listened for the music to begin. Then, syncing with the pulsing rhythm, I slowly rose by awakening one vertebra at a time. My body stood tall, unmoving, a solitary figure stretching toward the sky. With the rush of the melody, I spread my arms wide—shoulders back, chin high—then twisted across the floor in long, extended movements. I wanted to feel every part of my body extending and retracting to the music, which filled the studio with the same potency as the sunlight that poured through its windows. Some people were dancing for a grade. I was dancing in celebration.

Modern dance was much less rigid than the ballet classes I took as a little girl for ten years. Individuality was welcomed. Innovation was valued. Unique was the norm. My tummy was less of an issue here than it would have been in a class full of tall, pencil-thin dancers. It was the first semester of my sophomore year, and the course broke up a hectic day for a single mother and college student. I didn't care if I was getting every movement exactly right. It just felt good to *dance*.

And this was life now. A perfectly unchoreographed freedom dance. My feet were happy. At the grocery store, I tickled Nerissa as we walked the aisles, and we laughed too loud. At home, I sat at the computer all night writing papers while singing along to Lauryn Hill or Mary J. Blige. At the mall, I could even buy myself something—something small—without feeling guilty. In my little white station wagon, I zipped around Williamsburg with my hand out the window, feeling the wind rush through my fingers. In class, I soaked everything in as if it would all disappear—the professor, the class, all of the students, the whole college—at any moment.

The family-housing apartment wasn't supposed to come through. First, it was never intended to be a housing solution for an undergraduate with a baby. The assumption at William & Mary, was that a situation like that—a student like that—would never exist. But I found the loophole that didn't bar an undergraduate with a child from living there and filled out all of the paperwork. Later, as I help young parents overcome incredible housing challenges, I'll understand how rare it was for me to live in a dorm with my baby. My organization's research on student parents will find that, nationally, only 8 percent are aware of family housing options on their campus.[1] Second, I was placed on a waiting list. Even when supports like this are offered, the demand typically exceeds the supply. On the phone, the woman from Residence Life told me it wasn't likely I would get the apartment because a graduate student was slated to move in over the summer. I wasn't surprised; I had learned to expect and plan for the worst.

Expect and plan for the worst. Expect the doors to close and the answer to always be no. Plan for the worst possible outcome so that when it unfolds, you are ready. Live life in a constant state of *readiness*. Always be ready with a Plan B, and if it doesn't exist, create it. Quickly. My mantra was "Us against the world." Me and Riss, against the world.

I understand now that my decision to leave Rakheim and try to survive on my own as a single mother putting herself through college came in the wake of a storm—one of the most significant welfare reforms in our history. The Personal Responsibility and Work Opportunity Reconciliation Act of 1996 was a long, foreign string of words that I never saw or heard, and yet it influenced my life in so many ways. The sweeping changes were based on the fundamental idea that individuals, especially young mothers, on welfare, were taking advantage of the nation's cash welfare program, Aid to Families with Dependent Children. Conservatives painted a convincing picture of "welfare queens"—lazy single mothers, women of color, who were living off of handouts, with no incentive to work. The new system, the Temporary Assistance for Needy Families (TANF), instead required mothers to work or lose their benefits and left the states flexibility in how funds would be distributed and monitored. In 1993, Charles Murray's popular article in the *Wall Street Journal* paved the way for this type of legislation, stating that "illegitimacy is the single worst social problem of our time—more important than crime, drugs, poverty, illiteracy, welfare or homelessness because it drives everything else." The idea that young, single mothers were the most credible threat to our country was inescapable.

I was aware of the target on my back, like Hester Prynne's scarlet letter. I knew that people looked at me and assumed I was lazy and irre-sponsible. I felt the distrust and disdain everywhere I went. I felt it at the grocery store when Nerissa cried for candy and people looked our way. I felt it on campus when we walked across the lush green lawns to get our mail from the post office and other students wondered what we were doing there. I had felt it as I sat in the social services office in Newport News months before, trying to apply for food stamps. Attending college didn't count in determining my eligibility for food stamps—only work. The woman across the counter barely looked up from my paper appli-cation, making this crystal clear. I also didn't *look* like a college student. I was wearing Rakheim's oversized coat, large gold-hoop earrings, and a messy bun on the top of my head. And I had a baby.

I understand now that school didn't count because poor young mothers—specifically Brown and Black mothers—wouldn't, couldn't, or shouldn't go to college. School didn't count because the architects of TANF didn't think about certain key considerations when it comes to helping families move out of poverty. Yes, the number of welfare cases went down under the new system, but the poverty rate didn't. This means that no one was tracking whether the jobs that people were securing ac-tually paid enough to traverse over the poverty line or whether their employers offered benefits like health insurance or paid leave, which are necessary for family health and stability. They didn't address the barriers that often prevented mothers from keeping these jobs, like finding ade-quate and affordable childcare. They ignored the long-standing policies, systems, and biases that held back families of color from opportunities that could accelerate their success—like equal housing, access to quality schools, and fair employment practices. Instead they declared that only a mother's individual choices determine whether or not she lives in poverty.

But in the midst of the upheaval of a teenage pregnancy, I *chose* to go to college. I chose to go to one of the oldest and most prestigious colleges in the country. A college that had educated four US presidents, a secretary of defense, an FBI director, and countless CEOs and entrepreneurs. And I was there, raising my daughter, with few supports, and like the majority of students with children, with a higher GPA than some of my peers.[2] I sat in class some days surviving off of nothing more than a granola bar. I was hungry. I was trying. And yet, school didn't count. It was clear to me then, and still is now, that choices alone do not fully determine someone's status in life.

We received food stamps for a few months once they agreed to count Rakheim's hours at the shipyard toward the work requirement. When I took a part-time job as a cashier at Target the summer of my freshman year, they determined that our household income surpassed the threshold. I was "successfully employed," and our case was promptly closed.

My backup plan for the family housing unit was an apartment off campus that would be double the price. I had crunched the numbers one night while Rakheim was selling at King's Arms and Nerissa was asleep. I stared at my calculations on a small piece of notebook paper, wanting to find a mistake that would show me that living on my own was possible. Had I forgotten a grant or a loan? Maybe I had overestimated something? Was there such a thing as cheap infant childcare? A few days before I was supposed to go look at an apartment complex near campus, the call came. The woman from Residence Life told me the graduate student had a dog, and they didn't allow pets. She asked if I still wanted the unit.

"I'm going to warn you, it's not in good shape," she said, her voice flat. "You may want to go by and see it first."

"I'll take it," I said. "I don't need to see it. I'll take it."

On a humid August afternoon, Meron, a new friend I'd made on campus, and I drove over to the Ludwell dorm complex where the apartment was. We walked briskly up to the building, found the door on the first floor, and stood in front of it. I opened my hand to reveal the key. On the door, a shiny gold letter, "B," stared back at me.

"Open it!" Meron said, shaking my arm.

I inserted the key, turned it, listened for the sweetest sound of a click, and opened the door. Inside was a two-bedroom apartment with worn hardwood floors, a gas stove, and a tiny bathroom. There was a rear entrance in the dining room, and each window looked out at lush green Williamsburg trees. It was dusty and old, with a few cockroaches, hadn't been renovated since the 1970's, and was heated by radiators that sat by the windows in each room. In the winter, I'd find out that the radiators didn't work when the cold air seeped in. To help, the maintenance man would bring us a small space heater that would short a fuse if it was plugged in overnight, and I would miss my alarm for class in the morning. All he could do was offer a sympathetic smile through his thick graying mustache and say there wasn't much he could do since the building was about to be renovated. We had to settle for no heat during the week. On those nights, I would pull Nerissa into the bed with me and wrap us up in as many blankets as I could find to keep warm. I would tell her stories until I could feel her shivering stop, and the weight of her little body drift off to sleep.

I furnished the apartment with odds and ends. In the dining room, I used a table my grandmother had given Anika when she was at Yale. I covered it with a cheap flowered tablecloth from Target. I didn't have any chairs to go around the table so for a while, I didn't use it for anything more than a place to pile papers and mail. In the living room, my computer sat on top of my little desk. No couch. Just an oversized black leather chair that came from one of the crack houses Rakheim had frequented. The TV rested on top of a wooden crate. Nerissa's room was bare except for her crib, which was falling apart by now, and a used changing table. Just my bed, the dressers that Rakheim and I had put together from Kmart, and a hamper occupied my room.

When you have slept on people's floors, in cars, and next to someone who feels more like your enemy than your partner, you stand in the middle of your first apartment—no matter what condition it's in—turning slowly, holding a hand to your mouth in disbelief. After we were all moved in, I did that for a few minutes while Nerissa looked up at me smiling, her belly peeking out of her tight pink shirt with a yellow flower on it. That night, I watched her sleep next to me, her fat cheek gently squished against my pillow, and I cried. The tears were a mix of incredulity, gratitude, and an understanding of how close to the cliff we actually were. None of this was promised, and the entire responsibility of making sure it wasn't snatched away rested solely on my shoulders.

· · · · ·

Nerissa was over a year old now. She could walk and say, "Mama," "no," "hot," "hi baby," and "cracker." She loved cheese and would try to sneak into the kitchen to find a slice in the fridge. Mrs. Davis called her legs ham hocks because they were so thick. Her curly hair made a soft Afro around her head. When she laughed, her giggles made my heart jump and revealed two tiny teeth on her bottom jaw—the first to come in. I could see her personality coming through more and more. Silly, mischievous, and a greedy appetite for Mommy.

The daycare center wasn't supposed to come through either. Now that I was going to be living on my own in Williamsburg, Paula was no longer an option. I had to find reliable, affordable childcare—one of my most formidable obstacles.

Twenty years later, my first time speaking on Capitol Hill would be at a briefing championing a federal program that provides funding for colleges to create on-campus childcare for low-income students. It would serve only 1 percent of the millions of student parents nationwide,[3] and I would make the case that childcare solutions increase the likelihood that parents will graduate. But in 2000, campus-based childcare centers for students were almost unheard of. William & Mary's childcare center, the Williamsburg Community Child Care Center (WCCC), was a parent co-op on campus where all the professors sent their children. A white house nestled in the shade of Williamsburg's towering oak, crape myrtle, and catalpa trees, it was decorated with bright reds, blues, and yellows with floor-to-ceiling windows, a small cafeteria, and a sprawling, brand-new playground covered in fresh mulch. When I called to see if there was an opening, they said no, and my mom paid fifty dollars to put Nerissa on the waiting list. A week before I moved to Williamsburg, I received a call telling me they indeed had an opening. The tuition was $740 per month, but I applied for a scholarship for parents attending William & Mary and was only responsible for $320 per month for the first year. The scholarship ended after my sophomore year, and from then on, I was forced to pay full price.

Here in the summer of my freshman year, as a single mother with a one-year-old baby, a full course load, and no money, I *had* to find a way to make it. I had to pore over pages of information to find a loophole that could work in our favor, call every office not once but two and three times until someone would talk to me, and, like rearranging the pieces of a puzzle, find the basic necessities that we needed to live on to keep us going.

A Pell Grant and loans covered my tuition and our living expenses. We barely survived on roughly nine thousand dollars a year, and because there was no Pell Grant funding in the summer, those were the most difficult months. I couldn't work and go to school full time—not at a place like William & Mary and not without childcare in the evenings. Nerissa was still on Medicaid, but I was uninsured. My parents purchased the school's health insurance for me sophomore year for a total of six hundred dollars. The price went up during my junior year, so I paid for it myself with loans from then on.

The Special Supplemental Nutrition Program for Women, Infants, and Children (WIC), which provided limited nutritional food and formula after I stopped breastfeeding, was one of the only places I felt accepted. The ladies behind the counter loved to see Nerissa when I came every month to pick up my vouchers and a few items. At the supermarket, I learned how to buy the bare minimum for groceries, concentrating mostly on getting things for Nerissa, and then I would eat whatever was left over. We didn't go to restaurants. I made dinner at home, mostly spaghetti, Hamburger Helper, or drumsticks, and homemade cookies and pies when we could afford a treat.

I cut corners and budgeted as creatively as I could. I frequently had to call and ask for extensions on my rent or on Nerissa's daycare tuition. So many nights, I sat at the dining room table, looking at the numbers again, hoping I was missing something. I learned to just focus on the next twenty-four hours because anything more than that was too overwhelming. If I could get us through the next day and keep Nerissa fed, happy, and oblivious to the reality of it all, that was a success.

Even though these costs were difficult for me, they will be almost impossible for the young parents I will start working with in 2010. From the year 2000 on, the costs of attending college will skyrocket. At community colleges it will increase by 28 percent and at public universities like William & Mary, it will increase by 54 percent.[4] In 1971, tuition and fees at William & Mary cost $660 annually for in-state students. When I arrived in 1999, tuition and fees had increased to $4,610 per year. By 2020, tuition and fees will total $23,628.[5] This number won't include the costs of housing, books, travel, or food, which poses the very real question of whether I, as a young mother, could have graduated from William & Mary today with the same financial situation.

Visits from my mom were small welcome reminders of time when I did not have to be all things to anyone. A time when someone took care of *me*. When I opened the door, and she stood there with her arms open wide and her bright smile, she brought with her the warm, familiar feeling of just being together, out in the garden or on a walk around the lake near our old house in Virginia Beach. When she drove down from where they lived now in Northern Virginia to see the apartment for the first time, she took me shopping at Walmart to buy sheets, towels, and pots and pans. That Christmas, she bought me a futon that I could use as a couch in the living room, and I could finally throw away the big black chair that was falling apart. We'd cook dinner together on my tiny gas stove, bumping into each other in the galley kitchen while Nerissa watched *SpongeBob* or *Rugrats* in the living room. Then, when our bellies were full and Nerissa was asleep, we'd sit on the futon and talk like we used to.

She often told me how strong I was, and I'd shake my head, lips trembling because the memory of us holding each other on my bed the day I told her I was pregnant was still raw and because when you're working so hard to make it, you're sometimes afraid to recognize your own strength. But you need to hear someone say it. You need to hear someone say that you're strong. Later, when I am designing my program for teen parents in college, I will bake this into our DNA. Young parents—and any group of young people who have been pushed to the outskirts—need to hear someone say that they are strong, not just weak and vulnerable. I often tell our Scholars, a title we chose intentionally, that they can focus so much on becoming a college graduate that they forget how incredible they are *right now*. My mother was giving me this same gift.

. . . . .

I was also a college student. Between trying to pay the bills, making sure Nerissa was fed, bathed, and cared for, piecing together our meals, putting a Band-Aid on the constant oil leak in my car, and trying to coparent with Rakheim, I took six classes—fourteen credits—my fall semester. It was exhausting but necessary to graduate on time. Most days, I scrambled out of bed, fed Nerissa, and twisted her dark hair into small, sectioned braids before driving her to WCCC to drop her off for the day. Then, I would try to find a parking space along Richmond Road, which was one of two long stretches that ran parallel to the campus and met at a point right in the heart of Colonial Williamsburg. I could leave my car there for two hours at a time without getting a ticket. Most of my classes were on Old Campus, where the historic buildings of the College stood tethered to the Sir Christopher Wren Building—the oldest college building still standing in the United States. Tucker was a couple of doors down.

I had moved beyond the basic classes that were required of all students and was now taking courses that counted toward my English major. American literature from 1865 to 1920. I reread classics like *The Great Gatsby* and the poetry of Robert Frost, the words resonating with me much differently now as a mother who had been through so much than as a high school student. I didn't have much of anything, except a bare apartment, a computer, a stack of novels, and a beautiful little girl. Nerissa gave my life significance. I was important, even if only to her, and that was more than enough. The way she looked at me made me want to be the best version of myself and gave me an illogical optimism when I stood before an empty refrigerator or when I could barely keep my eyes open while I studied late into the night.

I reread *The Adventures of Huckleberry Finn*, and the story of Jim running to freedom in Ohio, not wanting to be sold away from his wife and children, also read differently this time. The realization that I was curled up reading this book on a campus that existed because of its reliance on the institution of slavery did not escape me. I could feel the presence of slaves who were purchased and brought there to serve college presidents and professors—never to learn or reach their own full potential. The college had even owned Nottoway Quarter, a tobacco plantation. For a fee, students could bring slaves with them when they moved onto campus to clean and run errands for them throughout the year. The echoes of this were still there. In 2000, less than 5 percent of the undergraduate student body was Black,[6] and as was the case at many colleges across the country, I saw more people who looked like me working behind the counters in the dining hall or maintaining the facilities than anywhere else on campus. I knew that many of them were probably young mothers, like me, or the children of young mothers, like Nerissa. I knew that this campus was not created for people like us, and I couldn't shake that recognition as I walked along the old red brick paths to class.

That semester, I took a Women's Studies class called US Women from 1600 to 1879, with Professor Maureen Fitzgerald. She was incredibly smart, referred to her partner several times during her lectures, and was one of the most down-to-earth instructors I had met at William & Mary. She was an academic, but she seemed like someone you could grab a sandwich at the Cheese Shop with too. She was passionate about women's history, covering every aspect, from every cultural perspective, reminding us of every bias—even our own. But even for someone so aware and enlightened, she wasn't prepared for a student to be in the situation I was in at William & Mary.

On the first day of class, Professor Fitzgerald asked each student to introduce themselves and share what they had done during the summer. Girls talked about safaris in Africa, trips to Europe with their families, internships on Capitol Hill, and archeological digs. A sinking feeling began to take root in my belly as I listened to each incredible answer. I knew I was different, but this exercise was showing me just *how* different I was from all of the other girls in this class. I tried to think of a way to make a brief summer job at Target saving up money to leave my daughter's father sound impressive. When it was my turn, I quickly mentioned my stint as a cashier, my face hot and red, and turned to the girl next to me.

Before she could introduce herself, Professor Fitzgerald interjected and said, "God, I love that store."

She liked me. She liked my comments in class, my writing, and once she found out that I was a single mother putting herself through school full time, she had a newfound respect for me.

"So how do you do it?" she asked, leaning back in her chair and tilting her head to the side one day, cleaning her blue wired glasses with her sweater. I had rushed to her small office to drop off my final paper by the noon deadline. She sat behind her desk, which was crowded with books like the shelves of several bookcases behind her.

"Do what?" I asked, standing in the doorway.

"How are you going to school with a child? And how old is she?"

Like most parents in college, I was careful about telling my professors that I had a child. More than 20 percent of students with children aren't comfortable sharing their parenting status at all; that number is higher for parenting students of color.[7] But Professor Fitzgerald seemed safe. Her opinionated lectures showed she felt motherhood was weaponized against women throughout history—treated as a disease, punishment, or a handicap instead of an asset and something to be celebrated. When Nerissa woke up one morning throwing up, I emailed her and told her my daughter was sick so I wouldn't be able to come to class. She wrote back immediately: "Wow. Of course. Come talk to me after the next class about making up the test."

Other professors weren't so understanding. Like my journalism teacher at Tallwood, the fact that I had a child was an inconvenience that wouldn't be accommodated. During freshman year, when Nerissa had pneumonia, my theater professor told me that I would have to bring her to class if I didn't want to fail. I bundled her up that morning, packed her into the car, drove to Williamsburg, walked with her across campus in the frigid cold, and made sure I was there at the start of class. The professor barely acknowledged Nerissa as she sat on my knee, whining now and then. After that, the professor treated me differently, more harshly. I mentally took note that my parenting status might affect my grades, not because I couldn't do the work but because some professors would simply hold it against me. This fear will understandably be shared by so many parenting college students I will meet over the years, contributing to their invisibility.

Professor Fitzgerald ran her hands through her short red hair and put her glasses back on, blinking a few times to determine if the smudges were gone. "Are you doing well in your other classes?"

"Yes. I am."

"That's a big deal," she said. "That's a really big deal. I hope to see you in another class. It's been a pleasure having you as my student."

I finished the semester with two B+s, two Bs, an A, and a "Pass." Despite trips to the emergency room for Nerissa's allergic reaction to penicillin and late nights rubbing frozen bananas on her gums to relieve her teething, I was doing the very thing people said I couldn't do and the thing *I* sometimes said I couldn't do.

· · · · ·

I still missed Rakheim. It was like weaning myself from a drug. I missed the good things, and somehow, I even missed the pain—the never-ending roller coaster of arguing and making up. I couldn't escape him. He called constantly—while I was in class or in the middle of the night. Usually he just wanted to tell me he needed me back and that things were bad without me. A couple of times he threatened to kill himself if I didn't come back to him. He might be drunk and high, crying into the phone, or completely sober. And I saw him every time I looked at Nerissa. Her full lips, her round face, and those deep brown eyes. Mrs. Davis always said he must have "spit her out."

He hardly asked to see her. That was the most surprising thing about leaving him. I thought he would want to be with Nerissa all the time. I couldn't imagine not being there for all of her milestones or just the little things, like her sleepily greeting me in the morning.

I now know that while I was immersed in a school setting with peers and a growing network, Rakheim was lost. He—like many young fathers—lacked something positive to keep him engaged and away from the streets. He didn't grow up with a role model for what a father was supposed to do and be, and he didn't have any role models now in his circle of friends. It would be another fifteen years before President Barack Obama would put this dearth of programming for young men of color on the national stage through his My Brother's Keeper Alliance. And it would be the agony of seeing Nerissa waiting by the window for a dad who seldom came that would solidify my commitment to ensuring young fathers have the supports they need to graduate from college and the freedom to be active in their children's lives.

But I didn't give in to Rakheim's constant pleas to get back together. When he called, I told him I had to go. I'd hang up the phone, and I wouldn't dial his number again to tell him I felt the same way. I'd cry into my pillow until the tears finally stopped. I'd go to sleep, hoping I wouldn't miss him so much in the morning.

The housing, the daycare, the new friends—none of it was supposed to come through. Each time I crunched the numbers on that piece of notebook paper at the dining room table in our old apartment, they crowded together to form an impossible, unsolvable equation that consumed my thoughts and conveyed to me that my only choice was to stay in an oppressive and turbulent relationship to survive. How many women stay with a partner who hurts them emotionally or physically because he is the primary breadwinner and because our systems are not set up for them to leave? How many women were in the same situation I was, but for them, the stars didn't align? The housing didn't come through. They never received the call about an opening at the childcare center. There were no family members who could pay for their health insurance. They didn't have transportation to get to the WIC office to buy formula. No one in their family had ever gone to college—or ever planted the seed that they could earn a degree. What happened to them? What happened to their children? What happened to their promise and their potential? The stars had aligned for me—for a reason.

I put one foot in front of the other each day. I danced my freedom dance. I relished the possibilities that were before me and Nerissa. The "welfare queen," the dean's list public ivy college student, Nerissa's mother, and our nation's greatest threat. All of me danced.

CHAPTER 12

TAKING SHAPE

TODAY, AN OXYGEN TUBE was wedged in Mrs. Davis's nose while she sat in the hefty brown reclining chair in front of the TV in the back room. The screen door and the open windows ushered in the cool damp April air to help with her hot flashes. Despite our hopes and prayers, the cancer was back with a vengeance. Each time she adjusted herself, her face twisted in pain and didn't relax until she was comfortable again. She was completely bald, and her face and body were swollen from the steroids. Her suffering was visible, yet in the midst of it, she told me to hand her a hair elastic, determined to teach me how to put twists in her grandbaby's hair.

Nerissa placed a chubby finger against Mrs. Davis's shiny brown head and told her she liked her haircut. We laughed for a while, and then, when Mrs. Davis pulled herself together, she motioned for Nerissa to sit between her legs. She was almost two years old now. Despite my feeling like I never had enough books at home or enough time to sit and play like the other parents at her daycare, Nerissa spoke so clearly, and she was catching on so quickly to shapes, colors, and the ABCs. Mama D called her an old soul. "You've been here before, haven't you?" she used to ask her as she cradled her in her arms. She sprayed Nerissa's thick black hair with a mist of water and told us she had decided that we weren't allowed to call her Mrs. Davis anymore: I should call her Mama D, and Nerissa should call her Grandma Davis. We both agreed.

I watched closely as she smoothed a glob of Ampro styling gel through the small section of hair that she gently held between her fingers. She explained that her mother had taught her how to do hair, and it wouldn't take long for me to master this easy style. As she secured the section with the black elastic, she asked me how I was doing. She wasn't talking about school. She wanted to know if Nerissa and I had what we *needed*. I already knew what the next question would be. She would ask what she always asked: When was I going to take Rakheim to court for child support?

Tammy Currie was right when she said that I could *survive* on my own. We were just surviving. Every day I was deciding between diapers and textbooks and food and rent, reworking the puzzle pieces to ensure that we could get through the week. When people question whether young mothers have the capacity to go to college, I will wonder if they understand the mental acrobatics that we have to perform in order to keep our families afloat—the magic we must spin. The intelligence, creativity, and ingenuity are boundless. Regular support from Rakheim—even a small amount—would have relieved some of this pressure, but he constantly had excuses for why he couldn't help. He didn't have the money right now. He was saving up for his own place. He had to give some money to Tina because the Neon was in the shop.

While I will meet many hands-on and supportive young fathers over the years, I will also meet so many young mothers who are scrambling, like I did, to provide for their children on their own—only 30 percent of teen mothers receive regular child support payments.[1] Sometimes it's because young fathers aren't established financially themselves, similarly lacking education and working low-paying, dead-end jobs. Sometimes it's because young fathers refuse to contribute or be a part of their children's lives, leaving mothers to bear the full financial burden. And sometimes it's because young fathers are entangled in the criminal justice system. Whatever the case, providing for a child on your own, without making good money, can feel like an impossible task.

When I gave birth to Nerissa, single motherhood was steadily climbing and at the center of a political battleground. In 1960, the US Census reported that 9 percent of children lived in single-parent families. By

2000, the year I left Rakheim, that number had climbed to 22 percent.[2] During the 1992 presidential campaign, Vice President Dan Quayle famously criticized *Murphy Brown*, a show about a recovering alcoholic and hardworking TV reporter who made a conscious decision to raise a baby on her own. He blamed the show for contributing to the breakdown of American family values in a speech that *Time* noted was "the most widely quoted speech of the presidential campaign." Ultimately, Bill Clinton, Democratic governor of Arkansas, defeated Quayle and incumbent Republican president George H. W. Bush, but the public and legislative attacks on single mothers continued, and more than twenty-five years later, about one-third of US children would be living with an unmarried parent.[3]

The issues of teen pregnancy and single motherhood are tightly intertwined. At the time that teenage pregnancy was defined as a major social problem, total birth rates among teens were actually falling steadily, but something else was on the rise: out-of-wedlock births.[4] There are many theories about why, but one is that the availability of legal abortions and more effective contraception in the late 1960s and very early 1970s made the need for "shotgun weddings," a union rushed by pregnancy to avoid embarrassment, obsolete. At the same time, the stigma associated with premarital sex seemed to lessen as a result of the new challenge of traditional beliefs. It wasn't that more teens were having children. In fact, in the 1950s, nearly half of all teenagers who were married were pregnant at the time that they exchanged vows.[5] Instead, more teens were *not marrying* as a result of their pregnancy. By the 1960s, there were fewer pregnant teens, but there were more single mothers.

To combat this trend, legislators berated single mothers, inaccurately declared teen pregnancy an epidemic, and vilified Black and Brown mothers, as opposed to addressing the root issues and the conditions that keep these families in poverty. Single mothers and their children are nearly six times more likely to live in poverty than married families.[6] Without a postsecondary credential, they typically work several low-paying jobs, still barely making ends meet. While more education would increase their earning power and outcomes for their children, less than a quarter of single mothers earn an associate or bachelor's degree, compared to 37 percent of married mothers. Investments in their educational attainment are inadequate and unpopular, particularly among those who purport to be strong advocates for children and families. As a young, Black single mother halfway through a four-year degree, I was not just an anomaly at William & Mary; I was an anomaly *everywhere*.

These days, I didn't even know where Rakheim lived. He moved constantly between Paula's and Tina's houses, staying with friends, and spent long stints at different hotels. Weeks would go by without a word from him. When we did talk on the phone, if I mentioned needing help paying for diapers or daycare, he asked for more time—maybe next month. But the help rarely came. In addition to knowing he didn't have a real job, I was hesitant to take him to court because I was afraid. I didn't want to jeopardize *his* survival, and, even more intimidating, I was afraid of what he would do. I wasn't sure if one hundred dollars a month was worth the possibility that he might become violent. Mama D watched me thinking through these things as she methodically spiraled the portions of Nerissa's rich black hair together and neatly curled the end around her finger.

·····

A girl named Audrey, whom I befriended in our many English classes together, told me she was getting her teaching certification with the hopes of working as a middle-school teacher when she graduated. If I was certified to teach, I'd be guaranteed a job. I decided to apply and was accepted into the two-year program in the School of Education. In addition to my final general education requirements and courses for my English major, I was also taking secondary-education classes now, and next year, I'd have to do student teaching on top of everything else. It was a lot, but Nerissa needed to eat, and that was all I could think about. I also applied for a paid internship through the Virginia Association of Broadcasters and was assigned to WVEC-13, an ABC affiliate in Norfolk, as a production assistant for the coming summer. I didn't know all of the research on single mothers at the time, but I knew that most of them didn't live a life like Murphy Brown.

I spent my days in class, my evenings feeding and bathing Riss, and my late nights studying until I fell asleep in my books. I hated group projects because they often forced an uncomfortable conversation about meeting times. I'd have to explain that I had a baby, and meeting at night would be difficult for me. Some of my classmates would be understanding and flexible while others were unbending. They'd insist on 8 p.m. meetings in Swem Library, which, like most college libraries, wasn't kid friendly. People soon knew me around campus as "the girl with the baby."

In May, right after my last final, I was able to move into one of the renovated buildings in Ludwell, a few buildings over from our first apartment, in Building 504. A couple of friends, Dede and Holly, helped me drag boxes and a hamper full of clothes through the parking lot, up the stairs, and into the new place. Brand-new linoleum floors, fresh wooden kitchen cabinets, smooth white countertops, and lots of light coming in through the windows. Best of all, there was a new thermostat to keep us warm in the winter and cool in the summer. I wasn't sure how I was going to pay the increase in rent, but I had to find a way to make it work.

With a small SpongeBob figurine in her mouth, Nerissa watched us bring everything upstairs then wandered off into the living room. When all of the boxes were inside, I put a frozen pan of lasagna in the oven, and Holly made some fruit punch Kool-Aid. We pulled chairs around the table and laughed at Rissa smearing noodles and sauce all over her face. The sun was setting, and the orange sky filled the apartment with a sleepy warmth that mirrored the feeling in my heart. To have food, shelter, a healthy child, and good friends was like a dream.

A few weeks later, Nerissa turned two, and I threw a birthday party for her in the new apartment. My parents drove down from Alexandria and helped me set everything up. My mom and I made little cupcakes that looked like umbrella beach scenes for our SpongeBob theme. Meron and the rest of my friends came back to campus from their parents' houses, where they stayed in the summers. Mama D drove up from Virginia Beach with two little girls from her church. Even Paula arrived from Portsmouth with her three kids.

While I held Nerissa above her birthday candles to blow them out and make a wish, Rakheim sat in a Norfolk jail. He'd called collect right after we moved into the new apartment, saying he'd been arrested for driving on a suspended license and needed bail money. I told him I had nothing for him, and after a few minutes of promising he'd pay me right back when he got out, he asked me to put Nerissa on the phone. The next week, my first week interning at WVEC, I had to go to the jail to investigate a case for an evening segment, and I decided to look up Rakheim's name in the database. In addition to driving with a suspended license and a cracked taillight, he had been charged with possession of cocaine and possession of a firearm. He stayed in jail for two months before getting off on a technicality and completing a couple of days of community service.

Understanding the experiences of teen mothers requires an acknowledgment of how the mass incarceration of Black men, backed by White oppression, has decimated Black families. In 2015, 44 percent of incarcerated youth will be Black, despite the fact that they only comprise 16 percent of all youth in the United States.[7] Young Black fathers will account for 30 percent of all incarcerated male teens, leaving young mothers and children to fend for themselves, often in poverty.[8]

Siera, a student in my program, has seen nearly every Black man in her life impacted by the prison system, including her father and the fathers of both of her daughters. Born and raised in South Carolina, a state with an incarceration rate that exceeds the national rate,[9] Siera describes a childhood with an alcoholic mother, a father who was constantly in and out of prison, a stepfather who started sexually abusing her when she was five, and a string of foster homes. She became pregnant with her first child at twelve years old after having sex with her seventeen-year-old boyfriend for the first time. She will admit that she was searching for someone to love and care for her.

"I hadn't had a period," she will say. "I could feel movement in my stomach. I was scared. I didn't understand. I didn't know what a trimester was. I didn't know about ultrasounds."

Hiding her pregnancy in a small town was nearly impossible, and soon people noticed her growing belly and began talking about her and shaming her. When she really started showing, at about five or six months, she was pulled out of school and forced to finish the year sitting alone with a teacher in the library. When she graduated from high school, she had a seven-year-old daughter. She had her second child at eighteen, after moving to DC to live with her aunt.

"Both of their fathers were in prison," she will say. "The only thing they could do was talk to them on the phone and send money from prison for us to eat if they could."

Her own father was released from prison five years before and lives in South Carolina. It's hard to visit, but they talk on the phone frequently: "He's an excellent father and grandfather. He has tried so many times to make up for lost times."

Despite the odds, Siera earned her associate's degree from the University of the District of Columbia Community College and is earning her bachelor's degree while also working. She lives with her daughter's grandmother, who helps her financially and babysits when she can, but she feels stretched in too many directions raising the girls alone. "Sometimes," she will admit, "I feel like I can't do this."

In 1965, President Lyndon Johnson gave the commencement address at Howard University and—pulling from the widely debated report *The Negro Family: The Case for National Action*, also called the Moynihan Report—provided a clear explanation for why Black families have not been allowed to thrive. "Perhaps most important—its influence radiating to every part of life—is the breakdown of the Negro family structure," he said.[10] "For this, most of all, white America must accept responsibility. It flows from centuries of oppression and persecution of the Negro man. It flows from the long years of degradation and discrimination, which have attacked his dignity and assaulted his ability to produce for his family."

· · · · ·

The question "Is college worth it?" will become more and more popular as time goes on. By the time I launch my organization, it will be a frequent headline in small and major news outlets alike. The definition of "worth" will focus solely on the economic returns for an individual who goes to college and whether their earnings will outweigh or offset the total costs of attendance. Of course, the question of the benefits of college won't be asked of well-off teenagers. It will be directed at people for whom the costs of college will be a stretch or nearly unfathomable— mostly people of color, including teen mothers and fathers. The answer is yes, college is worth it. In 2019, the Federal Reserve will find that the average individual with a bachelor's degree earns $78,000 per year compared to $45,000 for those with only a high school diploma.

This question will frustrate me not only because it seems to be searching for reasons to further exclude low-income and Black and Brown students from accessing the socioeconomic mobility that higher education brings, but also because it uses too narrow a definition of "worth." Martin Luther King Jr. arrived at Morehouse College when he was fifteen years old, three years later observing, "I too often find that most college men have a misconception of the purpose of education." While my hardships had transformed a degree into a simple means to an end, now at William & Mary, I was realizing, as King did, the college experience was so much more than that. Away from a toxic relationship, in the safety of our little home in the middle of Williamsburg's serene woods, surrounded by fascinating minds, college was affording me the space to listen, to find my voice, and to question the status quo.

Graduates of my organization's program years later will go on to pursue careers in computer engineering, education, social justice, public policy, business, and many other fields, armed with their degrees. They will make more money than they would have without their credentials, but the obvious sense of pride that they have when they come back to visit our office will stem less from their paychecks and more from a sense of self and an understanding that they have something important to offer the world. In addition to the monetary returns, college graduates are more likely to live healthier lives, volunteer in the community, and even vote.[11] College allows the space for individuals to learn who they are and use their uniqueness to change the world. Author and activist Chimamanda Ngozi Adichie captured this experience in her commencement speech at Wellesley College in 2015: "Please do not twist yourself into shapes to please. Don't do it. If someone likes that version of you, that version of you that is false and holds back, then they actually just like that twisted shape, and not you. And the world is such a gloriously multifaceted, diverse place that there are people in the world who will like you, the real you, as you are."[12]

It was fall 2001, the first semester of my junior year, and through writing, I was learning to untwist myself from the shapes that were designed to please others. The creative writing course was one of my six classes. We met in a small seminar room in Tucker, talking through structure and cadence and reading our stories aloud. Sometimes we did writing drills to get our thoughts flowing. The course awakened the little girl in me who used to fill whole notebooks, who used to consider writing as natural and necessary as breathing. I looked forward to every class, and when I proudly turned in my first short story, I couldn't wait to see if Professor Emily Pease liked it. She handed me the graded paper with a soft smile, her short blonde hair tucked behind her ear. She was in her late forties, pretty without trying to be, and always wrapped in cozy gray and brown sweaters. I rushed down the stairs gripping the story in my hand and planted myself under a tree in the Sunken Garden to read her comments. She loved it. It had a voice. It had intrigue. It had passion. It needed work, but it was a great start.

During one of my English classes, the professor announced that she was passing out information on the Honors English program as she dropped a piece of paper in front of each student. I straightened up in my seat and looked over the flyer. She went on to say that the program was highly selective and extremely demanding, but "if you feel that you have a burning desire to complete a year-long thesis your senior year, this is something you might want to consider." The thesis could be an in-depth study on a particular author or a genre or it could be an original creative work. It took me a couple of days to decide if I should apply. With student teaching, my senior year was already going to be hectic, but the opportunity to create a piece of work with the support of an advisor and a full literary review was calling to me.

I filled out the application and chose an advisor, Professor Pease. During our first meeting in a tiny cottage that she shared with another English professor just a few steps from Tucker, we went over the details. It would require a ton of reading over the spring and summer, and even if I made it to the point where I could submit my thesis, the project needed to be at least one hundred pages long. We did the math. That was approximately ten short stories. I'd have to take the Junior Honors seminar in the spring, and if I did well in the class, I'd have to write the proposal over the summer. I wanted the thesis to be a series of short stories about Black women during different periods in US history from slavery to the present.

Professor Pease emailed me a list of authors that she wanted me to study in preparation: Zora Neale Hurston, Alice Walker, Toni Morrison, and some male writers, including James Baldwin. I added my own: Ntozake Shange, Nikki Giovanni, and others. As we finalized the list,

Professor Pease warned me that even after I did all of that reading and put together a solid proposal, the committee might not even accept it.

That semester I made the dean's list.

· · · · ·

In an effort to stay out of jail, Rakheim started working as a pipe fitter at a construction company but still said he couldn't give me money each month for Nerissa. I applied for child support, and after he was served with the papers, he called me, furious. He yelled through the phone that I needed to call the child support office and tell them I wanted to retract the filing, that I had made a mistake. When I refused, he asked me if I wanted this to turn out like a Lifetime movie.

"You know what happens to those women in those movies, right?" he said. "Keep fuckin' around, and that shit's gonna happen to you."

The next time I saw him, we met at the mall in Chesapeake to pick up some spring clothes for Nerissa and then stopped at Kentucky Fried Chicken for lunch. While we ate, he tried to persuade me once again to drop the child support case by offering his tax refund instead. Frustrated by my refusal, he stood up with his tray in hand and lifted up his shirt to reveal a gun stuffed into the side of his pants.

"Why do you look so scared?" he asked with a smile.

· · · · ·

Only eleven people were admitted into the Junior Honors seminar and even fewer would actually go on to complete an honors thesis. I got an A- in the Junior Honors seminar and the approval to submit a proposal for my honors thesis at the end of the summer. I worked on it through each sweltering summer day and well into the simmering nights. I got a job making eight dollars an hour working at the business library that summer, hoping to make up for not having any loan money from May through August. It wasn't even enough to cover Nerissa's daycare tuition, so I was constantly apologizing for not having all of the money each month and asking for special payment arrangements. I lost twenty pounds as a result of being able to afford only enough groceries for Nerissa—applesauce, bread, juice, milk, and eggs—and averaged just a few hours of sleep each night, between caring for her and working on my proposal. Child support, which had finally come through, amounted to only $160 per month, barely making a dent in my expenses. When I begged Rakheim to help out more financially, his response was that Nerissa should just come live with him.

Within two years of earning my college degree, I will be a homeowner, and five years after that, I will be a CEO. The economic impact of my college degree will be certain. The less obvious but equally important outcome of my degree will be the opportunity to immerse myself in learning, and in my case, particularly in the wisdom of Black women, and to find my own voice in writing. And this love will always be a part of me. In my thirties, Nayyirah Waheed's words bubble over my soul and serve as a call to every pregnant girl who is deliberating her destiny:

> do not choose the lesser life. do you hear me. do you hear me. choose
> the life that is. yours. the life that is seducing your lungs. that is dripping
> down your chin.

CHAPTER 13

HONORS

THE BLACK CAP AND GOWN, the tassel draped over a proud, bright smile—all set against a sun-kissed day. I will love watching my students pose with their children for these photos, often teary-eyed. The picture represents the culmination of years of hard work and sacrifice—and proof that while every single one of them was told that they'd never go to college and they were ten times less likely to graduate because they were parents, *they did it.*[1]

I was just months away from my own graduation photo, crouched next to Nerissa in her blue-and-white sundress, holding a bouquet of red and yellow flowers in one hand and my diploma in the other, the two of us smiling in the bright sun. On that day, I will be floating, hardly able to believe I've made it, but there will be so many days just before it that will be daunting. My senior year will prove to be just as difficult as my freshman year—a trend that will ring true for the students I work with in DC. While many college completion efforts focus on college access, we will ramp up our check-ins and supports as our students get closer to their degree. A study in 2018 will find that nearly one in five students who leave college without a degree have completed 75 percent or more of the credits that they need toward their degree, and one in ten are as close as 90 percent.[2] My own experience taught me that as students near the finish line, life doesn't magically become easier.

This is what you don't see in a graduation photo.

My "time poverty" was at its worst during my final year of college. Each day seemed absolutely shredded between mothering, classes, student teaching, and writing an honors thesis.

My days started at 5:30 a.m. to get Nerissa fed and ready. I dropped her off on my way to Lafayette High School, arriving at 7 a.m., just before students trickled into my classroom. When the bell rang at 2:30 p.m., I'd rush back to campus for a class or a meeting with Professor Pease. Every night, after getting Rissa from daycare, I put dinner on the table, washed her up and brushed her teeth, read her a book, and kissed her goodnight. Then, I stayed up grading papers and exams, putting together lesson plans, and working on my thesis until I got to a point where I couldn't keep my eyes open anymore. I was averaging four or five hours of sleep each night.

I reached a breaking point with childcare. Like nearly one in five parenting college students, I was paying nearly two hundred dollars or more each week for childcare, more than the national average,[3] and I just couldn't do it anymore. One day in August, the director of WCCC pulled me aside and, in a hushed voice, told me she couldn't give me any more time to catch up on payments. I would have to pull Nerissa out of the program. The teachers hugged and kissed Nerissa goodbye and gave us an album filled with photos of memorable moments, including the annual Halloween parades to Baskin-Robbins. Because I had a feeling that Nerissa's days at WCCC were numbered, I had started researching other daycare options several months before. After searching online for hours for subsidized care, I found Williamsburg's Head Start program and called to ask about the application process. It required multiple trips to the Head Start office, copies of Nerissa's records, a letter from Tammy attesting to my financial status, and more phone calls to inquire about the status of my application. Thankfully, now that she was three years old, Nerissa qualified for the program as well as discounted before and after care. My daycare bill went from $700 to $44 each month. If Nerissa hadn't met the age requirement, or if there hadn't been an opening in the program, I would have been left without daycare just weeks before starting my senior year.

Even with a car, transportation continued to plague me. My station wagon was constantly in the shop. I couldn't afford to make the repairs to fix a constant oil leak, but with daily trips to Lafayette and Head Start, I also couldn't afford not to have a working car. I befriended a mechanic at a gas station on Richmond Road right by campus who was willing to do discounted fixes just to keep it running. I just prayed that it would last. A month before I graduated, the transmission died while I was going seventy miles per hour on I-64. I scraped together enough money for a small down payment, and my mom cosigned for a forest green 1993 Honda Civic at a dealership in Virginia Beach.

There was no coparenting with Rakheim. Not only was he still selling and often too drunk or high to even talk to Nerissa on the phone, he barely saw her, and he was becoming more and more erratic in his behavior toward me. It was as if he loved me too much and completely despised me all at the same time. He called me constantly, sometimes in the middle of the night, telling me he wanted me back and just needed to hear my voice. Other times, he threatened to "beat the shit" out of me if he couldn't pick up Nerissa when he wanted to. In the middle of class, I'd get ugly texts saying he was on his way to Nerissa's daycare to pick her up and that if I tried to stop him, he'd "put a bullet" in my head. I didn't feel safe on campus anymore or even at Ludwell. He told me he had ways of knowing where I was and what I was doing at all times, and one day, when I pulled into the parking lot behind my building, he was sitting in a nearby parking space watching me from his car.

I went to the local police department and showed an officer all of Rakheim's threatening texts on my phone. He scrolled through them, shaking his head, and told me that, unfortunately, there was nothing he could do. He suggested I go to the courthouse and get a protective order. Once I had that, if Rakheim violated it, the police could intervene. Three days later, I was at the courthouse for hours, trying to file a preliminary order of protection. I had to talk to several people at different desks before I finally ended up in the Commonwealth Attorney's office, where a representative explained the process and told me the order would be in place for fifteen days, after which there would be a full hearing to determine if there should be a new protective order in place, which could last up to two years. A large woman with short, graying hair sat in the middle of hundreds of pamphlets and brochures on domestic violence and looked over my file, shuffling from one paper to another. I asked her if she thought they'd ultimately grant me a protective order, while I glanced at a poster on the yellow office wall of a woman with a swollen, bruised eye staring back at me. It read, "Is this you?"

She said it wasn't likely that I would get the order. I emphasized that Rakheim had a gun and asked if I could show her the threats on my phone, but she put a hand up, signaling for me to keep my phone in my purse. She told me everything depended on which judge heard the case—each had their own leanings, sometimes toward the victims and sometimes toward the accused. When she said that there was a good chance the judge would throw out my case, I felt the panic filling my lungs. I imagined how enraged Rakheim would be by me taking him to court and how empowered he would feel if the case was dismissed.

"I know," she said after taking a deep breath. "I have women come into this office, and their husbands have shot them and stabbed them, and I think the case is a done deal, but you never know with these judges."

I looked down at my shaking hands. "I want to retract the papers."

In the parking lot, I crumpled up a brochure that she gave me, put my head against the steering wheel, and cried.

· · · · ·

There was something unexpectedly brilliant in all of this. I *loved* someone. I wasn't sure how it happened, and I didn't want to love him, but once it took root, it flourished and grew and couldn't be stopped. Without warning, his quiet affection curled in waves all over my body from my eyelashes to the soft spots behind my knees to the soles of my feet. He turned my skin into a rich soil so wherever he kissed me, a flower grew until eventually my whole body was alive like spring. After years of refusing to tether myself to someone for fear of their fallibility, it turns out, *he* was my place. My hand fit perfectly in his, and it will be the hand I hold before walking on stage to receive my diploma, while standing at the altar on our wedding day, and through the births of three more beautiful children.

Almost two years after I left Rakheim, I met Donté on the balcony of his friend's apartment before going inside to the loud party they were hosting together. I smiled up at him. A tall, thick defensive end on the Tribe football team, he could easily swing me over his shoulder in one swift move. Six-three and 250 pounds of goodness. He was the kind of guy who called his mother each week to check on her, stayed on top of all of his classes, and had an internship lined up for the summer. With jet-black neatly corn-rowed hair and smooth caramel-colored skin, he had a smile that was infectious, and no one made me laugh the way he did. He asked for my phone number that night so he could get to know me better. His next question, What time did I usually put my daughter to bed?, impressed me. So I wrote down my number on a piece of paper and handed it to him.

He wasn't my type. He was clean-cut, ironed his clothes, cooked his meals, and kept his room immaculately clean. I wasn't immediately head over heels, in part because he wasn't the kind of guy I was usually attracted to. My interest in him confused me—made me question what *my type* was. When my student Alicia tells me about her struggles with commitment and relationships years later, her description of the type of guys she usually dates will resonate with me. Their deficiency makes her feel useful: "I find guys who aren't doing as well as I am—guys who are mini projects. I feel like I can change them." Rakheim was my "mini project." He was only my type because he needed so much, and at that time, like Alicia, I was looking to fill my own voids by filling someone else's. Donté, on the other hand, didn't need anything, and I wasn't sure how to feel about that.

We had our first date a couple of weeks later. He came over on a Friday night after I put Riss to sleep, and we made my famous apple pie together, a recipe my mom passed on to me. We talked and laughed while thin, green Granny Smith apple peels flew every which way in my small kitchen, and he served as my sous-chef. He sang Motown oldies, and I laughed when his notes were off. I moved in a rhythm around him, reaching for ingredients in the cabinets, scooping peels off of the countertops, and washing bowls in the sink. I caught his eyes following me when I looked at him over my shoulder, and we laughed. I was so distracted I forgot to add a cup of sugar, but we sat on the futon with slices of pie and gobbled them up anyway. When he was done with his piece, he said thank you and kissed me on the cheek. I studied his kind face. I never knew feeling safe could be so romantic.

· · · · ·

The day I was unsuccessful in getting the protective order, I drove straight to Donté's apartment. I pulled into a space, then got out of the station wagon and leaned against the door, hoping to pull myself together before going inside.

"You alright?" I heard Donté ask from where he stood at his front door.

I looked at him with tears in my eyes.

"Come here," he said.

I earned an A in Ethics and made the dean's list again for the fall 2002 semester. I was so close to graduation now that I was ordering announcements, trying on my cap and gown, and filing all the paperwork, but I still had to make it through the spring.

My honors thesis was exactly one hundred pages long, comprised of eight stories about slavery, motherhood, maturation, marriage, hurt, and pain. Professor Pease and I edited it over and over until it was a polished piece of me. I gave copies to my three judges, one of whom was Professor Fitzgerald because of her expertise in women's history. Another was Professor Pease's office mate, who was known as an expert in African American literature and a harsh critic. They had three days to read it.

I walked into Professor Pease's small cottage, where the dissertation defense would be held. She offered everyone cups of tea, but I declined. I was too jittery and afraid I'd drop my cup and burn my leg. The manuscript sat on their laps, some of the pages scribbled on or earmarked. Their questions began right away. After two hours, they asked me to step outside while they made their decision. Professor Pease came with me, and when the door closed behind us, she assured me that I did great. I thanked her then smoothed my hands over my blue jeans, nervously, and looked at the Sunken Garden, sprawled out in front of us.

Four years ago, I'd come here wondering if I could even make it to senior year. Now commencement was only days away, and I could possibly graduate with honors. Our expectations for marginalized students are often the bare minimum, prescribing low expectations and precluding them from opportunities that could challenge them or reveal their brilliance. My thesis experience will convince me of the exact opposite—my expectations for my students will be high, and my assumption about their potential will be that it is limitless. And my students will prove me right time and time again—like Naraya who completed several semesters with perfect 4.0 GPAs and Yoslin, a DACA student, who will serve as a legislative intern for a state senator while working on her degree and raising her boys. Ana will earn a highly competitive nursing scholarship and secure a job at a local hospital before she even walks across the graduation stage.

That evening, I danced through campus, the rich, full trees watching over me and seeming to step aside as I walked through the doors of Swem Library, gripping a copy of my thesis. My stories would be preserved there—in a building I could never use, or use comfortably—in the university's archives, forever and always. I passed through the endless stacks of books and the sculptures and paintings in the library's art gallery to find the office, where a receptionist sat waiting for me. She took the manila envelope, looked inside, then sealed it back up.

"High honors, huh?" she said. "Congratulations."

I sat in William & Mary Hall, where my college journey first began, for the three-hour ceremony. In the graduation program that my parents held in their hands somewhere in the crowd, my name was listed as a bachelor of arts recipient with a distinction for high honors.

"And now, I officially congratulate the Class of 2003 as graduates of the College of William & Mary!" President Sullivan yelled from the lectern.

Black caps flew up in the air around me, and the hall resounded with clapping, whistling, and cheers. I spun around to take it all in. Joseph, who was told he was too dumb to go to college, will describe the feeling of this moment: "To just persevere, to walk across that stage and hear your name and hear people cheer for you—it was incredible."

Outside, there was a flurry of emotion and chaos as people poured out of the hall in search of one another. I found everyone gathered in a small group near the parking lot. Nerissa stood in the blue-and-white sundress that Mama D had given her, ready to hand me three big sunflowers. I rushed to hold her, scooping her up and crying into her chest. The day felt like it was *ours*. People will ask me what kept me motivated through every late night and every sacrifice, and it was Nerissa. I kept going because she needed me to, and now that I was a college graduate,

I could give her what I'd promised her in the delivery room the day she was born. This is the same answer I will hear from each of my students. Their children are their motivation.

"Happy Mother's Day," she said, handing me the sunflowers. "Are you done with classes now?"

We all laughed. Then I stood up and embraced my mother, who was beaming, trying to find the words to capture her joy and holding back tears. I held her tightly, not needing any words. The image of the two of us crying together on my bed in Virginia Beach five years before was fresh in our minds. Since that day, she had been my biggest cheerleader, sending money when she could, helping me strategize when I came up against an obstacle, and most important, embracing Nerissa and loving her unconditionally. When we pulled away, my dad patted me on my back, grinning ear to ear. "You're a college graduate, now," he said. In his own way, he was saying he was proud of me. Mama D stood to the side in her peach suit and matching hat and swung her arms around me, whispering, "Good job" in my ear. Donté kissed me and handed me a bouquet of the red and yellow flowers he'd been hiding in his car.

· · · · ·

I used to envision my graduation day when I sat in the Motel 6 as a way to help me make it through to the next day. When I pictured it, the scenes and faces were a blur, but now they were in front of me, each smile, wrinkle, and tearful eye exact and clear and just as it should be. Now I tried to envision what was next for me and Riss, and it was hard to think of an existence that didn't involve me functioning in a constant state of scarcity. I also couldn't imagine leaving my experience here in Williamsburg and not doing something for the millions of other young mothers and fathers out there who could do the very same thing and just needed the support and resources to get there.

I was about to fuel up my own rocket ship.

PART THREE

CROWNING

CHAPTER 14

INHERITANCE

HONEY. FOR A LONG TIME, that's the only name I had for her, and it fit. Her voice, soothing like honey drizzling over a piece of warm buttered toast, came through the phone every few months. As if she was reading a book or singing a hymn, she chose each word carefully while she asked me how school was going or told me that she thought of me often.

Through these phone calls and a handful of visits to our house, I thought I knew everything I needed to know about Honey. I knew that she lived in Daytona Beach in a house that my grandfather built for her a long time ago. I knew that she had a pecan tree in her backyard, and every now and then she would fill a box with the brown nuts and send it to us to crack them open and enjoy the rich, buttery flavor. I knew she used to bake delicious desserts, specifically, sweet potato pie and chocolate cake. I knew that she was my grandmother, and yet, I really didn't know her at all.

During my first and only visit to Daytona Beach, when I was twelve, I saw her house. It wasn't on the palm-tree-lined street I envisioned. It wasn't surrounded by other small well-kept homes with friendly neighbors who sat on porches sipping sweet tea while their children played. Honey's house, along with the rest of the neighborhood, was literally falling apart. The pastel-colored structures that used to be homes for the city's Black clergymen, postal workers, carpenters, and teachers were now hubs for drugs. When we stood on her porch and looked out at the street, my father talked about a community that once was, his eyes scanning the homes with a distant gaze.

The pecan tree was gone, and there were no homemade pies cooling in the window. Honey didn't cook much anymore. Instead, she shuffled through a small path through a sea of boxes that had overtaken her entire house to get to the kitchen, where she microwaved TV dinners or heated something in a pot on the stove. It was hard to believe that she was once a domestic worker—like the majority of Black women in Daytona Beach at midcentury, keeping other people's homes impeccably clean—as we tried to find places to sit among the clutter.

The details about my grandmother, whose real name was Annie Louise Hannans, are murky for many reasons. They will emerge in disunited and discontinuous stories when I'm much older and long after she has passed away. In 1930, Honey graduated from the high school department of what was then Bethune-Cookman College. In 1938, when she was twenty-six, unmarried, and pregnant with my aunt, she met my grandfather who was almost twenty years older and married to another woman. That meeting resulted in a years-long relationship and the births of my father and uncle. It lasted until my grandfather passed away forty-three years later. Honey was essentially a single mother raising three kids, and I will also learn that her oldest, my aunt, had her first child as a teen. During a rare phone call from her home in Jacksonville, my aunt will tell Anika that "teen pregnancy runs in our family." After poring over old records, I'll discover that Honey's mother, my great grandmother, had the first of nine children with her husband in 1905, when she was either twelve or sixteen years old.

In 2019, *The Atlantic* published an article entitled "The Consequences of Teen Motherhood Can Last for Generations" that prompted me to trace my own ancestral connections to single motherhood and teen motherhood. The article describes the conditions that significantly contribute to a teen pregnancy—poverty, family instability, limited opportunities—being entrenched in communities and families, not because of individual choices but because of larger systemic barriers. And this is especially true in communities of color. The article cites a study that finds "that having a grandmother who had her first kid as a teen is a strong predictor for whether a child will underperform in school—even for a child whose own mother gave birth as an adult, not a teenager." My mother and father weren't teen parents, but on my dad's side, these conditions were clear, holding back generation after generation from achieving their full potential.

When I discovered my pregnancy in high school, it felt like an isolated, singular experience in my family that was only connected to my individual choices and decisions. I considered myself an oddity because I didn't grow up hearing about Honey's life or about the lives of any of the other women in her family.

The family I knew very well, my mother's side, had a traditional mothering experience. Mémère was twenty when she and my grandfather married. The daughter of a Massachusetts dairy farmer, she hoped that the young man she met on the dance floor wouldn't notice her two left feet. She gave birth to my mother at twenty-five and stayed home to care for her baby while Pépère worked. His new job teaching chemical engineering at Yale came with a bigger home, a bit more money in their pockets, and two more children. They often entertained intellectuals over dinner, the air heavy with disregard for her input or opinion. She prepared lobster bisque and pound cakes to serve on her best china, hoping it might mask the fact that she didn't have a college degree or a driver's license. For the most part, their family embodied picturesque suburban life. While sexism was a way of life, Mémère seemed to relish providing a happy, stable home for her family.

Getting pregnant at seventeen without a ring on my finger was so different from Mémère's experience and from my mother's experience. It was, however, analogous to Honey's and her mother's. I imagine Honey's life was a daily task of shielding her children from their unique situation, from the looks and whispers of her neighbors and their community. I will feel connected to her—connected to her dire circumstances as a pregnant Black single woman in the South in the 1930s, connected to her lack of opportunities, her decaying neighborhood, her cluttered home, her constant need to protect her children from the world. And I will feel connected to her mother, Eleanyer, who was born in the aftershocks of slavery and just before *Plessy v. Ferguson* made racial segregation constitutional, ushering in the Jim Crow laws that further disenfranchised Blacks and reinvigorated

White supremacy across the South. She *existed* in trauma and *gave birth* in trauma. Neither went to college. Neither had a career. Being both Black and female, neither earned the wages they deserved.

These discoveries about my pregnancy within the larger context of my family coincided with my understanding of the plight of teen parents and people of color within the larger systemic conditions of our country. For me, the connections were no longer academic or uncertain. I had acquired the generational, inescapable ripple effects of poverty and oppression from Honey, Eleanyer, and the mothers before them, who will always be nameless to me, their legacies robbed and silenced by the institution of slavery. This was my inheritance, and it is the inheritance of millions.

 . . . . .

Over the years, I *chose* family, perhaps trying to fill the gaps of the fragmented line on my dad's side, and in the future, when I build my organization, I will create intentional space for our students to do the same, knowing that many of them will need to fill vacant roles with people who can walk with them in their college journeys. We will call them mentors, but they will play many roles—sometimes coaches, sometimes cheerleaders. Naraya will echo the importance of these individuals when she talks about her mentor, Trasi, and the absence of her mother, who died of lupus when she was fifteen: "I feel like in some sense my mom is kind of Trasi. My mom would have done what Trasi is doing, giving me that motivation to keep going and not give up."

Mama D was likely the Honey I never had—the strong Black mother figure who loved me fiercely and at the same time consistently delivered vital truths in her own brand of brutal, loving honesty. She had been a constant in my life for many years, each of our conversations or visits imparting a lesson in me, from how to season my vegetables to how to lean into my strength. Now she was dying, and even in this, she was teaching me humility and grace and service.

I stood in her living room, just before the two open French doors that led to the back room.

She probably should have been in bed, but she sat, stubbornly, in the brown reclining chair, with thin white sheets draped over her legs. Her face was so swollen there were very few hints of the Mama D I knew. Her eyes drifted behind her glasses, and her eyelids frequently lowered, too tired to stay open. I kissed her bald head, with light patches of gray hair here and there and swollen in places from the growing tumors underneath.

"Hey, baby," she said in a weak, childlike voice that made me choke back tears, then asked when I was bringing Nerissa, "her baby," by.

· · · · ·

A college degree is not a magic wand. The idea that hard work and educational achievement alone will completely reverse the socioeconomic conditions of young families and communities of color is both damaging and inaccurate. A 2015 study will show that White college graduates have more than seven times the wealth of Black college graduates and four times the wealth of Hispanic and Latinx college graduates. Even the households of White *single parent* graduates have twice the wealth of Black and Hispanic or Latinx college graduate households with *two* parents.[1] A degree cannot completely disrupt legacies of oppression. This type of intervention will require intentional policy changes across every system—financial, educational, correctional, human services, and so much more—as well as investments to address the gaps. As opposed to calling a degree a magic wand, my team and I will describe it as a "leveler" in the effort to overcome these disparities.

Two years had passed since I graduated from William & Mary. Time had added a few inches to Nerissa's height and taken away her two front teeth. When I looked down at my hands, I didn't see those pudgy fingers anymore. Instead they were long and slender—slimmed down by making lunches, giving baths, cleaning a house, working all day. I was still a single mother trying to make ends meet each day for Nerissa, but the circumstances were different now. I was navigating life with more options and more money, thanks to my degree.

Shortly after the commencement ceremony, my mind was singularly focused on securing a full-time job, not only because I had to quickly line up childcare but also because $30,000 in student loans was looming over my head. By 2020, the national student loan debt will climb to $1.6 trillion[2] due to increased costs and predatory lending that takes advantage of low-income families, and what will be lost in the student-debt crisis conversation is that Black student parents, typically mothers, hold more student debt than parents or nonparents of every other racial/ethnic background.[3] Overall financial need as well as childcare and living expenses will force them to borrow an average of $18,100, compared with an average of $13,500 among all students, $13,100 among White student parents, and $10,400 among Hispanic student parents.

Parenting students, who make up nearly half of all students attending for-profit colleges, institutions that similarly prey on low-income students with a promise of earning credentials quickly and moving into high-paying jobs upon completion, are particularly burdened by student debt. The average annual loans of parenting students at for-profit colleges are more than ten times higher than those of parenting students at community colleges.[4] Despite higher tuition, only 23 percent of students attending for-profit colleges graduate within six years, compared to 59 percent at public colleges and universities and 66 percent at private nonprofit schools.[5] This means that many parenting students rack up debt and leave school without a degree, often defaulting on their loans, and making it even more difficult for them to provide for their families. Racist policies have created a student-debt crisis that disproportionately impacts Black students, particularly those who are parenting, making them, as Tiffany Jones and Victoria Jackson write in the Education Trust series on Black student debt, "more likely to borrow, borrow more, struggle with repayment and default on their student loans than their peers."[6]

After graduation, I moved into my parents' guest room, this time sharing the futon with Nerissa, and spent every day applying for as many jobs and internships as I could. I landed an internship paying twelve dollars an hour at a boutique public relations firm in DC that would be the first of several corporate jobs I held over the next couple of years. These jobs would allow me to pay off my car, move out of my parents' guest room, and begin making payments on those student loans. After a couple of years in the private sector, I soon gravitated toward youth-serving nonprofits, where I could pursue my passions of working with young people and making a difference in the world.

· · · · ·

Donté and I were trying to figure out the balance in our relationship, both of us getting established in our careers—him in government contracting and me in nonprofit work—and purchasing our own homes while also spending time with Nerissa and potentially working toward a bigger commitment. He was a constant in my life, there for all of Nerissa's birthday parties, my graduation with a master's degree from George Mason University, and a move into my own townhouse. He was also there to calm me down after each chaotic exchange with Rakheim.

Even though Riss and I were now living in the DC area, I tried to make visitation work. I invited Rakheim to my parents' house and occasionally took Nerissa to see him down in Tidewater, but his threats, drunkenness, and unpredictability made it impossible. I was finally granted an order of protection for two years by a judge in Fairfax County, but after a year, Rakheim took me to court, and a different judge dismissed the order and granted him a visitation agreement. Donté was always there to pick up the pieces.

· · · · ·

I sat on the bus next to Nerissa the day after Mama D's husband called to tell me that she had died. We were taking a field trip with her class to a nearby farm, where she'd feed the animals, learn about how bees make honey, and pick out a pumpkin to bring home and carve. I was trying to hold myself together for her, but it felt like someone was sitting on my chest. I stroked Nerissa's soft black hair, which I had neatly pulled into four twists. The kids sang songs while the bus bumped along down winding roads in the middle of open fields, and I imagined Mama D was all around us.

CHAPTER 15

BREECH

AT SEVENTEEN YEARS OLD, Claudia was a teacher. She probably didn't see herself as one. She probably considered *me* the teacher and herself the student, and at the time, I saw our roles in that way too. But during our brief season together, Claudia taught me things about the realities of working with young people—things that I needed to understand.

I met her one evening at a small restaurant in Northeast DC for an event organized by a mentoring nonprofit that I had decided to volunteer with. When I had filled out my application, I had specifically asked to be paired with a DC public school student who was either pregnant or parenting. That wouldn't be difficult. In 2008, DC had one of the highest teen pregnancy rates in the country.[1] I stood holding a greasy vegetable egg-roll appetizer in a purple napkin while mentors mingled with their mentees. A woman from the organization came over to apologize and assure me that my mentee, Claudia, was on her way. In moments, she appeared in front of me wearing blue jeans and a leather jacket for the slight September chill in the air. She was petite with cocoa brown skin, an eager smile, and long, black braids down her back. Her swollen stomach was the only indication that she was pregnant. Everything else on her was tiny.

Our conversations were easy. She was friendly, smart, and eager to meet me, hoping I'd be "like an older sister." I was twenty-seven, which was still young enough for me to know the songs she was listening to and the TV shows she liked to watch. We discovered we both loved chocolate chip cookies and soul food and made plans to go out to eat soon. We talked excitedly about Senator Barack Obama's speeches and whether we thought he could *really* become the first Black president of the United States. She asked me if I was married when she saw the shiny, new diamond ring on my finger, which Donté had placed there almost a year before. She seemed to relax all over when I told her I'd been a teen mother. My daughter, I said, was now nine. Claudia lived with her mother and two older brothers in a row home near the Bolling Air Force Base in Southeast, Ward 8, a ward that accounted for the city's largest share of teen births—32 percent.[2] She was just starting her senior year at a charter school, and she was seven months pregnant.

When I picked her up for our first outing together, her mother, who looked like an older carbon copy of Claudia, stood in the doorway while I waited for her daughter to come downstairs. She took a puff of her cigarette then coughed and told me that the baby's father lived in the neighborhood and was "no good." He'd stopped going to school and was just selling drugs all day. She didn't think he was going to be in this baby's life.

Claudia seemed to have a different view of how things would go once she had the baby. When we were together, she was constantly glancing at her phone, anticipating his calls. She talked about her mother's opinions of him, rolling her eyes and saying that her mom was just being overprotective because when she had her brother at fifteen, his father abandoned her. The plan for graduating from high school after the baby was born involved him staying home with the baby while she went to school each day. She didn't have a backup plan.

When I asked to be matched with a teen mother it was in part because I considered myself an expert, given what I'd been through and accomplished. I envisioned swooping in with a big "TM" for "teen mom" on my chest, bestowing my wisdom. Each piece of advice would be gladly received and followed meticulously. My journey was a clear blueprint for overcoming the obstacles of young motherhood. All of this was, of course, ridiculous, and Claudia made that clear the first time I mentioned college to her. We were sitting in my car in front of her house, a gift bag full of brand-new baby clothes and supplies that I had just given her on her lap. Her son was weeks away from being born. Her shirts barely stretched over her stomach. She looked at me, perplexed, and said matter-of-factly that she wasn't going to college. She planned to work as a Metrobus operator, like her mom. No one in her family had ever gone to college. She was annoyed by me even bringing it up.

Over the next few weeks, our conversations instead focused on preparing for the baby. She called to ask if she really needed a Diaper Genie and if breastfeeding would hurt, because her mom said it would. She admitted one night on the phone that she was scared to give birth. She was scared of the pain.

· · · · ·

As I lay on my side just months after the conversation with Claudia, my arm and hand instinctively cupped my ripe belly. Tomorrow, I would be giving birth to a baby girl, who Donté and I had been praying for and planning for over the past year. We decided to try to conceive shortly after celebrating our one-year anniversary. For the first time, I was charting out my cycle, using a pregnancy app to determine when I was most fertile and really learning about my body in the process. Surprisingly, it took six months for me to see those two life-changing pink lines magically appear on the First Response stick in my hand. I took the test the morning of Donté's birthday so I placed it in a small gift box and wrapped it, presenting it to him "as a little something I'd picked up" for his special day before we went to bed. His reaction was shock and joy, bound together in a lingering bear hug.

Unable to sleep, I slipped out of our room in our townhouse and walked down the hallway to Nerissa's room to watch her sleep, something that always calmed me. Ten years old now, she slept wildly, twisted up in her covers. I stood over her, unable to imagine myself as anyone's mother but hers. So much was involved in taking care of her—doctor's appointments, parent-teacher conferences, attitudes and frustrations, hormones, basketball games, sleepovers, counseling sessions. People told me that my heart would expand when I gave birth to another child, but my heart had been completely consumed with loving Nerissa and trying to compensate for Rakheim's absences and deficiencies for so long, I wondered if it could get any bigger. And Nerissa's role would change within the family, too. She was going to be a big sister, a teacher, and a guide. I didn't know if she was ready for that; at times she struggled to just be happy with herself. I kissed her cheek then went back to bed. The train was coming.

Naya was breech, which meant she was trying to come into the world the wrong way—bottom instead of head first. One of the midwives confirmed this during an anatomy check of my belly at eight months along. I hadn't sought out a midwife. The obstetrics-gynecology practice I found when we moved to the new townhouse happened to have a large group of midwives who saw any expecting women who didn't have a high-risk pregnancy. I didn't know anything about midwifery, and neither did Donté. When we got in the car after the first appointment, when we saw Naya as a little gummy bear on the ultrasound screen, he asked skeptically, "Does this mean we have to give birth in our living room or something?"

We, like many in the Black community, were unaware of the long history of midwifery in Black culture, brought to America in the seventeenth century with African slave women. The practice of assisting childbirth was handed down from mother to daughter using African rituals and traditions, but Black midwifery suffered along with Black medicine generally at the turn of the twentieth century. Despite a gradual rise in the number of Black physicians in the early 1900s and newly established Black hospitals and medical schools, a single report by Abraham Flexner, published in 1910 by the Carnegie Foundation, helped to discredit Black medicine, shuttering all but two of the seven Black medical schools in the country. The message was loud and clear—Black medicine, including midwifery, was inferior. Flexner identified his alma mater, Johns Hopkins University, as the gold standard for medical care. We wouldn't be delivering in our living room. We'd be delivering Naya at the Johns Hopkins Hospital.

Everything about this pregnancy was different, not because Naya was upside down but because *I wasn't*. I was growing her inside me without the toxins that come from sleeping on floors and in motels, missing doctor's appointments, subsisting on Pop-Tarts, and facing these things afraid and alone. Instead, Donté was with me, and we were figuring things out, together, in our own imperfect way. In the operating room, his firm hand wrapped tightly around mine while we watched the doctor attempt to shift Naya into an upright position.

I will always struggle with trusting good things. Donté was a good thing, and for a long time, this struggle will rear its ugly head in our relationship. My student, Colleen, found a good thing, too. After she earned her associate's degree, she married a man she will describe as her best friend, someone totally different from her daughter's drug-addicted father. She will tell me, "He's my rock. He carries me with him." Donté was my rock. In the weeks after we brought Naya home, I had to remind myself to let him carry me. He took three weeks off of work to be home with us, cooking and cleaning, changing diapers, waking up with me for her feedings, taking Nerissa outside to dribble in the driveway. He was a father in every sense of the word, ready to watch a handstand or listen to an original poem, ready to give kisses and to tell each girl how much he loved them. And still, I had to remind myself to let him take care of us.

* * * * *

Claudia gave birth to a healthy five-pound baby boy named Timothy. The doctors predicted that he would be small, so we stocked up on newborn clothes and size-one diapers. I held him in her mother's living room a few weeks after he was born while Claudia looked on, smiling, from a chair in the corner. Her mother was smiling too. No one mentioned his father while they told me about her brief labor, running to the hospital in the middle of the night because her water broke in the bed while she was sleeping. Claudia said everything happened so quickly, it felt like he just "slipped out."

I talked to Claudia once more after meeting Timothy. I called her on a Sunday afternoon after texting her several times without a reply. I asked how they were doing. She told me she'd decided to give him formula, after all, and it seemed to be going fine. Her mother had insisted on getting the Diaper Genie, but she said, things were so hectic, no one had had time to set it up. We laughed. She admitted that she hadn't done any of the work her school had sent home so she wasn't sure she'd still be able to graduate on time. Between lack of sleep and not having any help during the day from Timothy's father, she didn't have time to get the assignments done. I told her that I could help her sketch out a daily schedule that might make it easier for her to get her work done and that she shouldn't take college off the table. She said, okay. After that, Claudia stopped returning my calls and texts.

I don't know if Claudia ever graduated from high school. I don't know if she ever went to college. I don't know if Timothy, who is likely in middle school now, has any relationship with his father. I don't even know if Claudia and her family still live in their rowhouse on a tree-lined street in Ward 8 where nearly 50 percent of the children are living in poverty.[3] Claudia's situation and the frustrations I had from my small role in it sparked a flame inside of me to *do something*. But there were some key insights that would influence the way I would go about it.

One, Claudia didn't want to go to college. I assumed, because of my own upbringing with college as a constant target, that *everyone* wanted to go to college. Claudia was working toward something different: a high school diploma and a necessary and respectable job as a Metrobus driver. Her aspirations were likely limited by not knowing anyone in her family or community who went to college or worked in a profession that required a college degree—things that are necessary for young people to know what is possible for them. But I should have been asking Claudia questions instead of making assumptions. What do you love to do? What do you enjoy? What do you do well? And if you could do something all day long, what would it be? Often, teen mothers, disconnected youth, and young people living in poverty aren't asked these questions. Instead, they're *prescribed* pathways. Claudia may have been passionate about following in her mother's footsteps, but maybe she wasn't. Maybe she needed someone to help her think through other possibilities. Either way, I needed to celebrate who she was and what *she* wanted rather than what I wanted for her.

Claudia saw college as completely unattainable. This was probably for a host of reasons. First, in Ward 8, only 16 percent of residents hold a bachelor's degree,[4] the lowest rate of any ward in the city. Growing up, college was a rarity, probably described as something reserved for other people with money and resources, which were equally rare in Claudia's neighborhood, or for talented athletes, who could secure a scholarship. After Claudia became pregnant, the prospect of going to college became even more implausible. When you are living in scarcity, there is little room or tolerance for daydreaming. Basic daily needs require realistic solutions. As a young mother, she needed to focus on the things that would feed Timothy and keep a roof over his head, not the things that were out of reach, like college. There were too many barriers to earning a credential after high school. My job—our job—is to clear the path and provide real solutions that remove barriers, making college feel less like a daydream and more attainable.

Claudia had some big hurdles to traverse before she could even think about college. There are short-term goals and then there are long-term musings. College was a long-term long shot that was hard to even talk about in light of what was happening in her life at that moment. This was a blind spot for me. Because I was so eager to have Claudia overcome the various obstacles in her life, I couldn't see the immediate obstacles that she faced, including just graduating from high school. Only ten years before, I had been in the same place, on the verge of disappearing from high school altogether, like Alexis and every other pregnant girl I knew— not because I didn't want to graduate but because my situation was so unstable, and I had so little control over what happened each day. I forgot how important it was to just meet Claudia where she was at *that moment* and make sure she had what she needed to get to the next step. We often push for the daydreams, ignoring the basic needs of young mothers and fathers that need to be addressed first.

Claudia needed to know how hard it was for *me*. I told her I'd been a teen mother, loved macaroni and cheese and candied yams, and simi-larly hung on every word of Senator Obama's campaign speeches, but she didn't really see me as someone who had made mistakes and struggled and suffered. By the time I met her, I held two degrees, was engaged, living in the suburbs of DC, and working as a nonprofit consultant and speaker. Regardless of the fact that I had gotten pregnant young, in her eyes, we couldn't have been further apart. She needed to see me as a human being who didn't have—and never had—all of the right answers. She needed to know how many nights I cried myself to sleep, how many days I went hungry, and how often—even at William & Mary—I doubted my ability to do any of the things I went on to accomplish. She needed to know that, even as I was mentoring her, Rakheim's volatile behavior toward me was taking its toll on my family. We need leaders who have lived through the battles of teen pregnancy, single parenting, poverty, "otherness," disconnection, and more—and we have to be courageous enough to talk about it.

· · · · ·

Not long after my last call with Claudia, on a blustery day in January, I watched former senator Barack Obama, the child of a teen mother, the first Black president of the United States of America, give his inaugural address. "Let it be said by our children's children that when we were tested, we refused to let this journey end, that we did not turn back nor did we falter; and with eyes fixed on the horizon and God's grace upon us, we carried forth that great gift of freedom and delivered it safely to future generations."

Donté sat beside me in bed that night, his hand resting on my belly, both of us filled with hope for his special birthday gift growing inside of me, bottom up, and for the promise of change that, in that moment, seemed inevitable.

CHAPTER 16

CEO

GLEAMING MARBLE FLOORS. Smooth emerald carpets. Massive mahogany columns. A buzzer positioned outside the door that no one hears the first time around. The office *smelled* like money—old, generational, legacy money—and, along with the people who worked inside it, felt impenetrable.

I sat in a chair across from the program officer at one of the city's major foundations with my best white blouse, freshly ironed black pants, and tall, black heels. We had already exchanged sweet stories about our children, my eleven-year-old and one-year-old girls, and her seven-month-old daughter, cherublike, blue-eyed, captured in several frames meticulously placed on her palatial desk. Now, she skimmed the overview for my organization, which I'd printed in a frenzy at home before jumping into the crawling early morning DC traffic, while I talked her through the major points. She was a new mother in her early thirties with a head full of brown chin-length spiral curls. She nodded and smiled as I stressed that no organizations in the DC area were currently helping more teen mothers and fathers become college graduates, speaking to the urgency of our work. It was just an informational meeting, made possible by one of our board members who was able to call in a favor for me to talk to someone at the foundation. Education wasn't even this woman's focus area. It was 2010, the year I founded Generation Hope. The Great

Recession had just ended, but unemployment was still at nearly 10 percent, and the foreclosure crisis was still robbing people of their homes.[1] We had no money, no office, and no employees. People said it was the wrong time to launch an organization.

The program officer told me that my personal story was impressive and my concept for the organization seemed well thought out. She wondered about the mentoring component, though. I planned for our mentors to not only volunteer their time, providing emotional support and encouragement as young parents worked toward their degrees, but also to put dollars toward their tuition. She wondered how realistic that was since she saw so many organizations struggle just to recruit mentors who would be willing to donate their time, never mind their money. Also, she said, the needs of this population were so significant that that might deter people as well. These were things that I might want to rethink. Years later, another program officer will suggest that instead of encouraging teen parents to earn four-year degrees, I should point them to certificates and trades, which are "more realistic paths for this population." For many people, my vision for an organization that would exclusively focus on college for young parents was far-fetched and idealistic.

I always thought that one day doing the big things would make me feel sure, comfortable, and 100 percent right—that sitting in an office like this with the stakes so high would at some point be easy. In my mind, the fear I felt as a girl, a college student, and even a young professional when confronted with any test or obstacle came from not being strong or savvy enough. I needed more practice, more polishing. I had done these enormous things, but in the midst of each of them, I questioned myself. When I left my parents' house, I had doubts about my decision and its impact on my future. At William & Mary, there were always moments when I felt crazy to think I could graduate and that feeling lingered, even as I walked across the stage to receive my diploma. Every time I stood in a courtroom with Rakheim over a visitation dispute or to secure another order of protection—even with Donté's hand on my back—my knees shook as I recounted the threats, drug dealing, and fascination with guns. I envisioned that one day, in the face of these types of challenges, I would reach a point where I'd have little hesitation, only assurance and clarity.

In a perfect world, this program officer would have seen the clear need for my organization, read the statistic in the first paragraph that less than 2 percent of teen mothers get a degree before age thirty, and made a small initial investment to help us get the work started, to seed this innovation. In a perfect world, she would have seen me—a Black woman with lived experience and a connection to the people I aimed to serve in a field where less than 20 percent of CEOs and executives are people of color—and considered me an *expert*.[2] Ideally, she would have asked me how she could help and who else I wanted to meet so she could make introductions. But none of that happened. She congratulated me on my work thus far, shook my hand, and asked to stay in touch.

It would take five years and several grant proposals before we would receive funding from that foundation, and ten years later, I am still experiencing the very real challenges of fundraising as a Black nonprofit leader. In the DC region, less than 3 percent of overall giving goes to organizations led by leaders of color,[3] and nationwide, it's less than 10 percent.[4] For a Black female leader, the numbers are even worse. In 2016, despite launching some of the most effective local and grassroots solutions, only 0.6 percent of foundation giving went to women of color.[5] But I wasn't launching Generation Hope in a perfect world, and really, that's why it needed to exist—because of all of the world's imperfections.

· · · · ·

Generation Hope came to be during a time when change felt inescapable. President Obama, who looked like me, raised by a young single mother, had just signed the most significant healthcare reform since the passage of Medicare and Medicaid in 1965, expanding coverage to some forty-five million people, disproportionately people of color. The Patient Protection and Affordable Care Act required employer-provided health insurance to cover birth control as a preventive service, expanding women's access to contraceptives. It allowed young people, including college students, under the age of twenty-six to stay on their parents' healthcare plan. Insurance companies would no longer be able to deny coverage based on preexisting conditions, such as pregnancy. Six years later, his successor—a man whose divisive policies will revive White supremacy and oppressive legislation across the country—will make it his mission to undo all of this progress, but for now, even in such economic uncertainty, President Obama made us feel like we could change *the world*. He seemed to be living the words he spoke so eloquently on the campaign trail: "And where we are met with cynicism and doubt and fear and those who tell us that we can't, we will respond with that timeless creed that sums up the spirit of the American people in three simple words—Yes, we can."

It began early one March morning in front of my computer. The night before, Donté had asked me an important question—the culmination of an hours-long conversation at our kitchen table over a pile of bills. Together, we had been crunching numbers, calculating and recalculating how—with me being unemployed and with us having two children and a mortgage to pay—we were going to make things work. My consulting job with Healthy Teen Network, a national reproductive health organization based in Baltimore, had been abruptly cut short as a result of the economic downturn. In a few weeks, we would be surviving solely on Donté's income as a government contractor, and the numbers didn't add up. I knew this frantic race to connect the dots and stay afloat well. It had been years, but the instinct to craft solutions and construct backup plans instantly kicked in. I was soon so immersed in this familiar routine that I almost forgot Donté was there. He gently covered my hand with his and met my eyes, then asked, "What do you feel like God is calling you to do?"

I made a joke about God wanting me to help him pay the bills, and we laughed, but he wasn't willing to let it go. He leaned back in his chair and asked it again, bringing us back to a place I found much less comfortable than making jokes or coming up with quick fixes. He wasn't asking me to come up with a solution for our immediate need. He was inviting me to *dream*.

That night, long after Donté drifted off to sleep next to me, I prayed for clarity. What *was* God calling me to do? And if it was something big, was I ready to answer?

• • • • •

What if we said yes instead of no? That was the guiding star in the design of our program. Yes to tuition assistance. Yes to helping you keep the heat on in the winter or fixing your car. Yes to having someone in your corner who believes in you—and let's make it multiple people. Yes to diapers and baby wipes and laptop computers for class. Yes to connecting with other young people who are going through the same things you are—parenting, working, and going to school. Yes to having a champion when you are caught in a never-ending bureaucracy, and while we're at it, let's commit to never creating unnecessary barriers to our own supports. Yes to having someone to talk to, including a mental health professional. Yes to career connections. Yes, you are deserving. Yes, you are special. Yes, you are smart and full of potential. Yes, the world needs you. Yes to being loved and accepted and celebrated. Just. As. You. Are.

I was unencumbered by restraints and norms. I didn't ask how much something would cost. I asked what the benefit would be if we made those investments. I didn't identify one issue and ignore the others. I tried to consider the totality of what I knew about being young and pregnant and try to solve for as many hindrances as possible. In addition to writing a check for tuition, we had to also address the isolation of being a pregnant girl or a teenage boy with a baby on the way. I didn't settle for surface solutions. I dug for the root causes. I tried to anticipate and offer services before a student had to ask for them—one less thing they'd have to think about in their busy days. I believed that if we removed the barriers that teen parents face by providing targeted resources and designing an entire organization with their experience in mind, we would see success. I came to describe it as wanting to be the place that says "yes" when everyone else says "no."

These ideas flooded each page. Hours later, I placed the period at the end of the last sentence then put the finishing touches on what would become our business plan, then our program model, and then our case for support.

· · · · ·

I was excited when we received the first application. It felt like Christmas. We'd spent the previous year meticulously laying the foundation of the organization—recruiting our board of directors, filing articles of incorporation, and earning our 501(c)(3) status. We had been talking about our students in hypotheticals for so long. Now, I was eager to actually "meet" a young parent and begin walking with them in their college journey. I ripped open the manila envelope and skimmed her written responses, but my excitement faded as my eyes found a date on the form that didn't make sense. She was seventeen and about to graduate from high school, but she had gotten pregnant at eleven years old and gave birth to her first child at twelve. She was just a child. Just a *girl*.

Teen pregnancy is complex and riddled with ugly truths that we often don't want to face. We want it to be simple, but it's not. When I speak to audiences about our work, a question that is almost guaranteed to come up in the crowd is: Why aren't we focusing on prevention instead of supporting teens who make bad choices? I have several responses to that question, but what I find most effective is sharing stories.

I might talk about our very first applicant, who, like Siera in my program, had little control of her situation or her body at such a young age. I will wait as a hush and a quiet fall over the crowd, people processing their assumptions about who *deserves* help and who doesn't. Or sometimes I tell them about Ariel, one of the fathers in my program, who is raising two young children and working and going to college along with his wife. When he talks about his experience as a husband and parenting student, sharing a stage with former First Lady Michelle Obama and other higher-ed advocates, he says he is doing this for his kids: "I feel it in my heart, I know that college will be a big part of their lives as well." Or I will talk about Siera, who spent too much of her childhood in foster care and sees a very simple future for herself as a college graduate: "I've never had a home. I've been bounced through foster care. My children have been bounced through foster care. I want a home. That's my goal. I want my children to not have to worry about being moved. That's what I see in my future. A place to call home. It doesn't have to be big, or fancy, it just has to be ours."

I didn't do this work alone. From the start, I surrounded myself with incredibly smart, passionate, good people who cared deeply about the mission and about our families—many who had been touched in some way by teen pregnancy, teen parenting, or single motherhood. I will continue to execute this strategy as the organization grows. A nonprofit executive herself, Meron was one of our founding board members; my mom and dad sat in the first row at every event and celebrated every milestone; and so many other friends and family will rally behind this cause. Donté will be an unofficial board member, with our meetings taking place over dirty dishes as we clean the kitchen after dinner or on long road trips with the kids asleep in the back seat. He will listen and encourage and give advice all while growing his own contracting business.

Although it will take four years to transition from a volunteer CEO to earning a full salary, by 2020, we will grow to a talented staff of nearly twenty, operate out of an office in DC that will include a family-friendly study area for our students and their children, and leverage a multimillion-dollar budget to champion for young families. We will work with hundreds of teen mothers and fathers attending twenty different two- and four-year colleges across the DC metro area. We will intentionally call them "Scholars" because they are so much more than the markers that others may have given them—"dumb," "dropout," "absent father," or "pregnant girl." In 2010, no one was talking about teen parents in college or parenting college students, but as the years go by, we will be both a part of and a leader in the student-parent movement. We will bring our Scholars to lend their voices in major forums at the Aspen Institute and Capitol Hill briefings to amplify the needs of what others will call nontraditional college students—those students who are parenting, working while going to school, students over the age of twenty-five, and students who do not have a traditional high school diploma. These groups actually comprise the college *majority*.[6] In 2018, recognizing that our Scholars' children deserve the best chance at their own academic success, we launched an early childhood program that provides everything from developmental screenings to monthly monetary support to help them access high-quality childcare and preschool programs.

Our results will disprove the pervasive myth that teen parents aren't capable of becoming college graduates. While half of parenting students across the country leave school without a degree, 90 percent of Generation Hope Scholars stay in college from year to year and 70 percent maintain a GPA of 2.5 or higher each semester, with some earning perfect 4.0s.[7] Our six-year graduation rate is higher than the national graduation rate for *all* college students, regardless of whether they have children, more than double the graduation rate for parenting college students across the country,[8] and nearly eight times the graduation rate for single mothers nationwide.[9] Ninety percent of our graduates are living above the federal poverty line within six months of graduation, and nearly 30 percent are enrolled in a graduate program within six months of earning their bachelor's degree. Over the years, we will listen to our students' feedback to enhance our services, adding mental health counseling, career-readiness supports that cater to the needs of parenting students, tutoring, and a robust early childhood program. Though research shows that the children of teen parents enter kindergarten at lower levels of school readiness,[10] by the end of the first year in Next Generation Academy, 93 percent of our children are on track with age-appropriate communication, problem solving, and motor skills. These are the traditional measures of effectiveness, but my favorite barometer for how well we serve our families isn't graduate rates or GPAs; it's how they feel about being a part of the Generation Hope family.

"One of the things I love about Generation Hope is that I'm not alone. Having tons of girls, even guys, with the same story. You can tell someone you were fifteen when you got pregnant, and there is no judgment. Generation Hope is a comfortable place to just be yourself," says Kathy.

"It's not just a scholarship. It's the fact that I can talk to anybody at any time. I feel accepted. I feel I belong here," Chelsea adds.

"With Generation Hope, I felt like people had my back, through text messages, phone calls. I felt motivated again," says Ariel.

"Trying to figure out how to feed your child makes you feel more and more less than. It makes you feel like you're always going to be in this category—unworthy. Below. Low. Poor. Especially when you come from poor. But Generation Hope sees you differently," notes Nija.

And Naraya told me that "Generation Hope literally saved my life. I would be a statistic right now [without GH]."

· · · · ·

In 2013, William & Mary featured me on the cover of their alumni magazine for my work with young parents in college. The next year, I will cry in the parking lot of Naya's preschool when a CNN producer calls to tell me I have been named a CNN Hero. In 2018, George Mason University will name me one of their top-fifty exemplar alumni, and I will receive the national Roslyn S. Jaffe Award for my work with women and children. In 2019, Trinity Washington University, the alma mater of Speaker of the United States House of Representatives Nancy Pelosi, will present me with an honorary degree and ask me to serve on their board of trustees. These accolades will feel as much like my students' accomplishments as mine, as much like wins for every young mother and every single mother who has ever been told they weren't worthy. They will be for my grandmother, Honey, and my great grandmother, Eleanyer, and the nameless mothers before her.

But what I will be most proud of is the small part we will get to play in the lives of amazing young people, most of whom never considered themselves "college material." They will do all of the hard work, staying up late, sometimes working forty hours a week and then going to school at night, waking up in a homeless shelter and heading to class, or escaping an abusive relationship to graduate magna cum laude. We will walk with them along the way, doing the small things, like greeting them with hugs in the office or reaffirming the agency and expertise they have in their lives, and sometimes we will do the much bigger things. I will love celebrating *them*.

And somewhere along the way, we will all realize that change demands a louder voice, that addressing the ingrained injustices that keep young parents from thriving and succeeding will require larger agendas targeting root causes and systems that need to evolve. We now recognize that we have to build on our work with families and engage the birth-through-high-school, human services, and higher-ed systems to make sweeping advancements that replace barriers with investments that accelerate the success of young families and parenting college students. We have begun to work closely with our partners at the Institute for Women's Policy Research; the Hope Center for College, Community, and Justice; the Aspen Institute's Ascend Program; the Annie E. Casey Foundation; the ECMC Foundation; the Seldin/Haring-Smith Foundation; and Imaginable Futures to advocate for and amplify our common goals. We have collaborated with Senator Cory Booker and Congresswoman Jahana Hayes on family-centered legislation while holding others accountable, requiring bold leadership that listens to the wisdom of mothers, faces the ugly truths, and leans into effective, unconventional solutions. Ten years after launching Generation Hope, I will be named one of thirty-one inaugural awardees of the national Black Voices for

Black Justice Fund to recognize my work to address structural and systemic racism in America. We pay homage to those who fought before us and stand in solidarity with organizations and advocates who continue the fight on behalf of teen parents, single mothers, Black and Brown families, today's college students, and the young people others leave behind.

. . . . .

I never reached that day when I faced the big things and didn't question myself. I will come to realize that if I reach that point, I'm probably not doing anything big. I'll always approach a microphone with butterflies in my stomach and ask for people's input when I have to make a far-reaching decision. But the one thing I will never do again is question whether I *belong* at the table.

CHAPTER 17

PEACE

I AM UPSTAIRS IN OUR BEDROOM, finishing up the message in Nerissa's birthday card when she pulls into the long driveway, so long it feels like its own street. I can hear her music blaring from the speakers, typical for a twenty-one-year-old, alerting me that she has reached the point where it curves to the left, right outside of our garage. At the window, I watch her park under the crab-apple tree that the kids love to climb. It is at its peak, in vibrant bloom now, and soon the soft pink petals will cover the ground beneath like a coral carpet.

We live on an acre of land at the end of a cul-de-sac on a quiet street lined with trees that seem tall enough and old enough to remember a time when there was nothing here but woods and farms and plantations. I often think about what these trees have seen when we sit outside on the front step to watch the children play or take a walk along the bubbling creek in the back to search for fish and turtles. I wonder if, as they sway in the quiet breeze, they wonder how we got here—how *I* got here.

We are a family of six now. Naya is a ten-year-old artist, with long legs, a kind heart, and endless energy. In the fall, we go door-to-door in the neighborhood selling cookies for her Girl Scouts troop, and in the spring, we give her encouraging thumbs-up from the bleachers during her volleyball practices. Donté Jr. came into the world four years ago, and his brother, Drew, followed two years later. Together, they are an unbridled tornado of joy, mischief, and destruction with a singular daily goal of going outside to pick up sticks, dig for worms, and occasionally eat leaves. They emulate Donté, wanting to ride behind him in their miniature John Deere tractor as he cuts the grass, but they love Mama, too. And Nerissa is a bright, fun, and busy young woman now. She's a senior at Towson University, majoring in business and marketing, cheering at football games, and navigating the frustrations of college roommates. She has her own relationship with Rakheim, separate from me, and I'm there whenever she needs advice for maneuvering his occasional upheavals.

Donté knows I'm happiest when we are all together. He says he can look at me and see how full my heart is, even during chaotic dinners with food on the floor and someone singing too loudly and multiple conversations going on all at once. I love the energy and the rhythm of this family. It is the heartbeat of our house, and Donté and I keep it going. The two of us have been together for nearly twenty years and married for nearly fourteen. We're a good team, figuring everything out as we go, just as we always have, making some mistakes along the way. Even after all this time, he is the only person I want to retreat to at night and the only person I want to wake up to in the morning.

Soon, my mom and dad will be here. They now live just fifteen minutes away. They attend every basketball game, birthday party, and play at school. My mom even volunteers at Naya's school. She and Nerissa are close, and Naya and the boys love to paint with her, just like I used to, in the studio at her house. Donté's parents will be here, too, driving up from their home thirty minutes away. Mrs. Lewis will be holding a warm tray of her famous corn pudding, lovingly prepared, at Nerissa's request. She will greet us with a hearty embrace and an infectious grin while the boys hug her legs. Donté is likely to be taking the hot dogs and ribs off of the grill downstairs. When it's warm, I can always find him on the deck, checking the meat as it sears on one side. He often leans on the wooden railing to look out at the thick green trees that surround our house. It is our first single-family home—our own little slice of the world—and I've told him many times I don't think I could ever live anywhere else.

I'm tethered to this place and to these people. My soul is anchored here. No matter how far away I travel, this is where I belong. This is where my heart is most full, and this is what I was really fighting for all those years. When I ask my students what they see when they envision their future, they don't describe fancy cars or high-paying jobs, they talk about *this*. Regardless of what the house looks like or how long the driveway is, we want the peace that comes from giving our children a home where they feel safe and loved and connected. This is the heart song of every mother I know.

I have to finish the card that I'm holding in my hand. I scribble the last few, simple words, "I love you," before sealing it and heading downstairs to greet her at the door. Donté and I make it a point to say these words to each of our children every day, multiple times a day, during a tickle fest or as we send them out into the world. We know that they, like the generation before us, will have much to overcome, but this is the one assurance that we can give them—that they are loved and that we will face each and every hardship together.

This assurance is what every child, every young person, and every human being needs and *deserves* in order to thrive. Without it, we are lost to the way the world defines us and the future it assigns to us, never reaching our full potential. Never realizing that while there is so much to overcome, we are more than just "a failure," "a problem" that needs to be solved, or "the pregnant girl." When we are loved rather than shamed, embraced rather than ostracized, championed rather than stifled, we have a better chance of catching the falling beads and stringing them carefully and methodically back together, creating a necklace that is more beautiful than before because it now reveals the exquisite, incalculable force that has been there all along.

ACKNOWLEDGMENTS

LEADING UP TO THIS POINT—this book—I have benefited from the love and support of a village. I was able to include some of the people from that village in these chapters, and others I must thank here.

I'm starting with Donte, my husband, my love, because after nearly twenty years together, you are still my best friend. Thank you for never being shocked by me receiving an award or a grant or even the publishing deal for this book. Your confidence in me is infectious and makes me look at myself in the mirror differently every day. And thank you for keeping our children at bay while I worked away on this manuscript. Thank you to our children—Nerissa, Naya, Donté Jr., and Drew—for serving as my ultimate inspiration to make the world a better place, which is my hope for this book. I love each of you infinitely. To my parents, Albert and Nancy Hannans, for always encouraging my love of writing and for instilling in me a bullheadedness to pursue my dreams. There would be no college degrees, no book, and no Generation Hope without that. And thank you to my mother and father-in-law, Doris and Sylvester Lewis, for your constant love and support.

Some acts and gestures have been big and others a bit smaller, but they have all added up to make this book possible. Thank you to Acacia Evans, Jennifer Brimmer, and Kaity Smith for bringing me groceries in Virginia Beach when I was pregnant and didn't have food to eat. Thank you to Lisa Young and her mother for throwing a baby shower for me when so many people had walked out of my life. To the lovely, smart, and talented women who welcomed me with open arms when Nerissa and I came to William & Mary and who are now like aunties to my children: Kia Weeden, Holly Smith, Wura Atkinson, Dede Pearson, Tamika Batten, and Katrina Jones. To my "ride-or-die," Meron Mathias, thank you for loving me and Nerissa from the start and for always being in my corner—no matter what. I remember you cried when I handed you the first draft of this book. And to Victoria Vickers and Marina Matthews (rest in power) for encouraging me to write about my experiences way back in 2004 during our days working at GEICO.

Then there are the many people who helped me lay each brick for Generation Hope and who continue to make it a joy and an honor to do this work every day. Kendria Thomas, thank you for helping me think through our programming over sushi and many late nights. Kimberly Korbel, thank you for writing the very first check to Generation Hope in 2010, and thank you to all of our founding board members for believing in my vision. Thank you to Jack Benson and the Reingold team for lending your expertise to a woman with a dream. Dr. DeRionne Pollard and Terri Freeman, you both saw what Generation Hope *could be* instead of what it *was*, and I can't thank you enough for that. To my current board of directors, thank you for your support and for doing the hard things that lead to true change. Thank you to my entire staff. You do the *real* work every day. And special thanks to my leadership team: Reginald M. Grant, Caroline Griswold Short, Ericka Best, Katherine Eklund, and Portia Polk. Thank you to the many mentors, volunteers, donors, and funders who rally around our mission and make it all possible. I don't take any gift, grant, or hour of your time for granted. To our students and graduates, thank you for allowing Generation Hope to be a small part of your incredible journeys, especially the Scholars and alumni who bravely shared their stories in this book: Alicia, Chelsea, Joseph, Kathy, Siera, Ariel, Naraya, Ana, Yoslin, Nija, and Colleen.

And to the people who truly made *Pregnant Girl* come together. To my mentor, Rebecca Linder, for being you and for introducing me to the amazing Aaron Kissel, who then introduced me to Jeff Nussbaum, who then introduced me to my fabulous literary agent, Joanne B. Jarvi. Joanne, it took me thirteen years to find you, but when I did, you took a chance on me and on this book and have become one of my biggest cheerleaders. To Helene Atwan and the entire Beacon Press team, thank you for lending your time and talents to this project. It has been an amazing ride. And thank you to my publicist Angela Baggetta for helping us amplify a story that has been silenced for far too long.

And if you've finished this book, you know that God connected many, many dots for me—making a way out of no way—and I have to thank him for that.

Lastly, the artist Frida Kahlo once said, "Nothing is worth more than laughter. It is strength to laugh and to abandon oneself, to be light." Thank you to every person who has made me laugh over the years, especially in the most difficult moments. It has made all the difference.

NOTES

CHAPTER 1: THE FIRST BEAD

1. "Racial and Ethnic Disparities Continue in Pregnancy-Related Deaths," Centers for Disease Control and Prevention, September 5, 2019, https://www.cdc.gov/media/releases/2019/p0905-racial-ethnic-disparities-pregnancy-deaths.html.

2. United States Census Bureau, https://www.census.gov/quickfacts/attleborocity massachusetts, accessed September 1, 2020.

3. "About Teen Pregnancy," Centers for Disease Control and Prevention, March 1, 2019, https://www.cdc.gov/teenpregnancy/about/index.htm#:~:text=In%202017%2C%20the%20birth%20rates,highest%20among%20all%20race%2Fethnicities.

4. "National Data," Power to Decide, https://powertodecide.org/what-we-do/information/national-state-data/national, accessed September 1, 2020.

5. Linda M. Burton, Marybeth Mattingly, Juan Pedroza, and Whitney Welsh, "Poverty: State of the Union 2017," Stanford Center on Poverty and Inequality, June 2017, https://inequality.stanford.edu/publications/pathway/state-union-2017.

6. Terrell Jermaine Starr, "STUDY: More Than Half of Black Girls Are Sexually Assaulted," *Newsone*, December 2, 2011, https://newsone.com/1680915/half-of-black-girls-sexually-assaulted.

7. "Statistics," Me Too Movement, https://metoomvmt.org/statistics, accessed September 1, 2020.

8. Raquel Reichard, "What Rape Culture Looks Like in the Latino Community," *Latina*, December 18, 2015, http://www.latina.com/lifestyle/our-issues/rape-culture-examples.

CHAPTER 2: WOMEN'S WORK

1. Teen Center: Dating Violence Technical Assistance Center, *Teen Pregnancy, Parenting, and Dating Violence*, issue brief, no. 8 (October 2009), https://www.breakthe cycle.org/sites/default/files/pdf/ta-issue-brief-10-09.pdf.

2. *The Facts on Adolescent Pregnancy, Reproductive Risk and Exposure to Dating and Family Violence*, Family Violence Prevention Fund, February 2010, https://www.future swithoutviolence.org/userfiles/file/HealthCare/adolescent_preg_facts.pdf.

CHAPTER 3: LOVE SONG

1. Ibram X. Kendi, "The Greatest White Privilege Is Life Itself," *Atlantic*, October 24, 2019, https://www.theatlantic.com/ideas/archive/2019/10/too-short-lives-black-men /600628.

2. "Leading Causes of Death—Males—Non-Hispanic Black—United States, 2016," Centers for Disease Control and Prevention, September 27, 2019, https://www .cdc.gov/healthequity/lcod/men/2016/nonhispanic-black/index.htm.

CHAPTER 4: TWO PINK LINES

1. Heather D. Boonstra, "Teen Pregnancy: Trends and Lessons Learned," Guttmacher Institute, February 1, 2002, https://www.guttmacher.org/gpr/2002/02/teen -pregnancy-trends-and-lessons-learned.

2. "Teen Abortions," Child Trends, 2018, https://www.childtrends.org/indicators /teen-abortions.

3. Diana Reese, "The Mental Health of Teen Moms Matters," Seleni Institute, March 14, 2018, https://www.seleni.org/advice-support/2018/3/14/the-mental-health -of-teen-moms-matters.

4. "Postcard: Teen Pregnancy Affects Graduation Rates," National Conference of State Legislatures, June 17, 2013, https://www.ncsl.org/research/health/teen-pregnancy -affects-graduation-rates-postcard.aspx.

CHAPTER 5: INTO THE DARK

1. *New York City Youth Count Report 2017*, City of New York, Mayor Bill de Blasio, https://www1.nyc.gov/assets/cidi/downloads/pdfs/youth_count_report_2017_final.pdf.

2. Terrence McCoy, "Inside the Hidden World of Homeless Teen Mothers," *Washington Post*, April 27, 2015, https://www.washingtonpost.com/local/inside-the-hidden -world-of-homeless-teen-mothers/2015/04/24/15b479f8-e868-11e4-9767-6276fc9 boada_story.html.

3. Diane Whitmore Schanzenbach, Ryan Nunn, Lauren Bauer, Audrey Breitwieser, Megan Mumford, and Greg Nantz, *Twelve Facts About Incarceration and Prisoner Reentry*, Brookings Institution, October 21, 2016, https://www.brookings.edu/research /twelve-facts-about-incarceration-and-prisoner-reentry.

4. Sendhil Mullainathan and Eldar Shafir, *Scarcity: Why Having Too Little Means So Much* (New York: Times Books, 2013).

5. Safiya Charles, "Demoralized and Disconnected: Black Girls Are Being Pushed Out of Schools. Here's How," *Montgomery Advertiser*, December 27, 2019, https:// www.montgomeryadvertiser.com/story/news/2019/12/27/black-girls-pushed-out -schools-ayanna-pressley-act-juvenile-justice-reform/2662361001.

6. Terry O'Neill, Bonnie Grabenhofer, and Chitra Panjabi, "Girls' of Color Educational Needs Are Equally Critical to Those of Boys of Color," National Organization for Women, May 7, 2015, https://now.org/resource/girls-of-color-educational -needs-are-equally-critical-to-those-of-boys-of-color.

CHAPTER 6: RED

1. "Miscarriage," March of Dimes, November 2017, https://www.marchofdimes .org/complications/miscarriage.aspx#:~:text=For%20women%20who%20know% 20they,1%20to%205%20percent)%20pregnancies.

2. Mindy E. Scott, PhD, Nicole R. Steward-Streng, MA, Jennifer Manlove, PhD, and Kristin A. Moore, PhD, "The Characteristics and Circumstances of Teen Fathers: At the Birth of Their First Child and Beyond," June 2012, https://www.childtrends.org/wp-content/uploads/2013/03/Child_Trends-2012_06_01_RB_TeenFathers.pdf.

3. Melissa Jenco, "12% of Teen Girls Report Reproductive Coercion," AAP News, October 1, 2019, https://www.aappublications.org/news/2019/10/01/healthbrief 100119.

CHAPTER 7: PLACE

1. Boonstra, "Teen Pregnancy."

2. Ellen J. Kennedy, "On Indigenous Peoples Day, Recalling Forced Sterilizations of Native American Women," *MinnPost*, October 14, 2019, https://www.minnpost.com/community-voices/2019/10/on-indigenous-peoples-day-recalling-forced-sterilizations-of-native-american-women/#:~:text=Between%201907%20and%201939%2C%20more,were%20carried%20out%20in%20California.

3. Michelle Kessel and Jessica Hopper, "Victims Speak Out About North Carolina Sterilization Program, Which Targeted Women, Young Girls and Blacks," Rock Center via the *Black Women for Wellness Blog*, November 7, 2011, https://www.bwwla.org/victims-speak-out-about-north-carolina-sterilization-program-which-targeted-women-young-girls-and-blacks.

4. Saudi Garcia, "8 Shocking Facts About Sterilization in U.S. History," *Mic*, July 10, 2013, https://www.mic.com/articles/53723/8-shocking-facts-about-sterilization-in-u-s-history.

5. Timeline/Renewing Native Ways, "1976: Government Admits Unauthorized Sterilization of Indian Women," July 17, 2015, US National Library of Medicine, https://www.nlm.nih.gov/nativevoices/timeline/543.html.

6. "Women of Color Need Improved Information and Access to Effective Contraception," Bixby Center for Global Reproductive Health, February 1, 2014, https://bixbycenter.ucsf.edu/news/women-color-need-improved-information-and-access-effective-contraception.

7. *A Historical Report of Opportunity*, Opportunity Nation and Measure of America, 2011, https://opportunitynation.org/history-of-opportunity.

8. *Helping Young People and the Economy to "Be Great,"* Boys & Girls Clubs Within Los Angeles County, August 2010, https://www.smbgc.org/wp-content/uploads/2015/08/Economic-Impact-Study_LA-Aliance_Sept_2010.pdf.

9. Georgia Perry, "Silicon Valley's College-Consultant Industry," *Atlantic*, December 9, 2015, https://www.theatlantic.com/education/archive/2015/12/silicon-valley-college-consultants/419538.

10. *Increasing College Opportunity for Low-Income Students: Promising Models and a Call to Action*, Executive Office of the President, January 2014, https://obamawhitehouse.archives.gov/sites/default/files/docs/increasing_college_opportunity_for_low-income_students_report.pdf.

11. Stephen Burd, "New Data Reveals, for First Time, Each Colleges' Share of Rich Kids," New America, April 8, 2017, https://www.newamerica.org/education-policy/edcentral/rich-kids.

CHAPTER 8: A SOUL MELTING ON HOT PAVEMENT

1. "Race, Drugs, and Law Enforcement in the United States," Human Rights Watch, June 19, 2019, https://www.hrw.org/news/2009/06/19/race-drugs-and-law -enforcement-united-states#_B._Incarceration.

2. Jenae Addison, "How Racial Inequity Is Playing Out in the Opioid Crisis," *PBS NewsHour*, July 18, 2019, https://www.pbs.org/newshour/health/how-racial-inequity -is-playing-out-in-the-opioid-crisis.

3. "More Funds Needed for Opioid Abuse," Assemblymember Diana C. Richardson, Assembly District 43, https://nyassembly.gov/mem/Diana-C-Richardsonvideo /7898/#videos, accessed September 1, 2020.

CHAPTER 9: THE STRENGTH IN BETWEEN

1. Stephanie Hanes, "Teenage Pregnancy: High US Rates Due to Poverty, Not Promiscuity," *Christian Science Monitor*, May 22, 2012, https://www.csmonitor.com /The-Culture/Family/Modern-Parenthood/2012/0522/Teenage-pregnancy-High-US -rates-due-to-poverty-not-promiscuity.

2. Warner Hessler, "Michael Vick," *Daily Press*, April 21, 2001, https://www.daily press.com/news/dp-xpm-20010421-2001-04-21-0104210156-story.html.

CHAPTER 10: ALL GOOD THINGS

1. Sara Goldrick-Rab, "High School Wasn't Always Free, So Why Are We Still Paying for College?" *Medium*, December 16, 2016, https://timeline.com/when-high -school-wasnt-free-f436fd1eeebd.

2. Generation Hope, *Uncovering the Student-Parent Experience and Its Impact on College Success* (May 2020), https://static1.squarespace.com/static/50363015e4b09af 678ee8675/t/5ebb60b839793d1dee21ee12/1589338301092/GH_%23StudentParent Success+Report_single+pgs_Final.pdf.

3. Madeline St. Amour, "Working College Students," *Inside Higher Ed*, Working College Students, November 18, 2019, https://www.insidehighered.com/news/2019 /11/18/most-college-students-work-and-thats-both-good-and-bad#:~:text=The%20 Georgetown%20report%20found%20that,to%2026%20percent%20in%202012.

4. Jon Marcus, "Student Advising Plays Key Role in College Success—Just as It's Being Cut," *Hechinger Report*, November 13, 2012, https://hechingerreport.org/student -advising-plays-key-role-in-college-success-just-as-its-being-cut.

5. Melissa Emrey-Arras, *More Information Could Help Student Parents Access Additional Federal Student Aid*, Report No. GAO-19–522 (Washington, DC: GAO, August 2019), www.gao.gov/assets/710/701002.pdf.

CHAPTER 11: FREEDOM DANCE

1. Generation Hope, *Uncovering the Student-Parent Experience and Its Impact on College Success*.

2. Lindsey Reichlin Cruse, MA, Tessa Holtzman, Barbara Gault, PhD, David Croom, and Portia Polk, "Student Parents by the Numbers," Institute for Women's Policy Research, April 11, 2019, https://iwpr.org/iwpr-issues/student-parent-success -initiative/parents-in-college-by-the-numbers.

3. Melissa Emrey-Arras, "More Information Could Help Student Parents Access Additional Federal Student Aid," Report No. GAO-19-522 (Washington, DC, GAO, August 2019), www.gao.gov/assets/710/701002.pdf.

4. Sara Goldrick-Rab, *Paying the Price: College Costs, Financial Aid, and the Betrayal of the American Dream* (Chicago: University of Chicago Press, 2016), 2.

5. "Historical Data 1971–2000," William & Mary, https://www.wm.edu/offices /financialoperations/sa/tuition/historical-tuition-data/history/index.php, accessed August 6, 2020.

6. "E02: Fall Headcount Enrollment (1992 thru Current Year)," State Council of Higher Education for Virginia, https://research.schev.edu/enrollment/E2_Report.asp, accessed August 6, 2020.

7. Generation Hope, *Uncovering the Student-Parent Experience and Its Impact on College Success*.

CHAPTER 12: TAKING SHAPE

1. Planned Parenthood Federation of America, *Pregnancy and Childbearing Among U.S. Teens*, June 2013, https://www.plannedparenthood.org/files/2013/9611/7570 /Pregnancy_And_Childbearing_Among_US_Teens.pdf.

2. Pew Research Center, *Parenting in America: Outlook, Worries, Aspirations Are Strongly Linked to Financial Situation* (Washington, DC: Pew Research Center, December 2015), https://www.pewsocialtrends.org/2015/12/17/1-the-american -family-today.

3. Gretchen Livingston, "About One-Third of U.S. Children Are Living with an Unmarried Parent," Pew Research Center, April 27, 2018, https://www.pewresearch .org/fact-tank/2018/04/27/about-one-third-of-u-s-children-are-living-with-an -unmarried-parent.

4. George A. Akerlof and Janet L. Yellen, *An Analysis of Out-of-Wedlock Births in the United States* (Washington, DC: Brookings Institution, August 1996), https://www .brookings.edu/research/an-analysis-of-out-of-wedlock-births-in-the-united-states /#:~:text=And%20the%20disappearance%20of%20shotgun,both%20white%20 and%20black%20women.&text=If%20the%20shotgun%20marriage%20rate,as%20 much%20as%20they%20have.

5. Frank F. Furstenberg, *Destinies of the Disadvantaged: The Politics of Teen Childbearing* (New York: Russell Sage, 2007), 9.

6. Lindsey Reichlin Cruse, MA, Jessica Milli, PhD, and Barbara Gault, PhD, *Single Mothers with College Degrees Much Less Likely to Live in Poverty*, Institute for Women's Policy Research, July 30, 2018, https://iwpr.org/iwpr-issues/student-parent-success -initiative/single-mothers-with-college-degrees-much-less-likely-to-live-in-poverty.

7. *Black Disparities in Youth Incarceration*, Sentencing Project, September 12, 2017, https://www.sentencingproject.org/publications/black-disparities-youth-incarceration.

8. Natalie Brito, Rachel Barr, Jennifer Rodriguez, and Carole Shauffer, "Developing an Effective Intervention for Incarcerated Teen Fathers," Georgetown University and Youth Law Center, San Francisco, CA, Zero to Three, May 2012, https://elp .georgetown.edu/wp-content/uploads/2016/02/Britoetal2012ZTT.pdf.

9. "South Carolina Profile," Prison Policy Initiative, https://www.prisonpolicy.org /profiles/SC.html#:~:text=South%20Carolina%20has%20an%20incarceration,than %20many%20wealthy%20democracies%20do, accessed August 7, 2020.

10. Lyndon B. Johnson, "Commencement Address at Howard University: To Fulfill These Rights," June 4, 1965, in *Public Papers of the Presidents of the United States: Lyndon B. Johnson, 1965*, Vol. 1 (Washington, DC: Government Printing Office, 1965), 635–40, available at http://web.mit.edu/21h.102/www/Primary%20source%20collections/Civil%20Rights/Howard_Commencement.htm.

11. Philip Trostel, "It's Not Just the Money: The Benefits of College Education to Individuals and to Society," Lumina Foundation, October 14, 2015, https://www.luminafoundation.org/files/resources/its-not-just-the-money.pdf.

12. "Chimamanda Ngozi Adichie Addressed the Class of 2015 at Wellesley's 137th Commencement Exercises," https://www.wellesley.edu/events/commencement/archives/2015/commencementaddress.

CHAPTER 13: HONORS

1. Claire Wladis, "Many Student-Parents Drop Out Because They Don't Have Enough Time for Schoolwork, Research Shows," Hechinger Report, July 24, 2018, https://hechingerreport.org/opinion-many-student-parents-drop-out-because-they-dont-have-enough-time-for-their-schoolwork-research-shows.

2. "Emerging Benchmarks & Student Success Trends from Across the Civitas," Civitas Learning, Spring 2018, https://www.insidehighered.com/sites/default/server_files/media/Civitas_Community_Insights_Spring2018_VF.pdf.

3. Sara Goldrick-Rab, Carrie R. Welton, and Vanessa Coca, *Parenting While in College: Basic Needs Insecurity Among Students with Children* (Hope Center for College, Community, and Justice, May 2020), https://hope4college.com/wp-content/uploads/2020/05/2019_ParentingStudentsReport.pdf.

CHAPTER 14: INHERITANCE

1. Michaela Broyles, *A Conversation About the Racial Wealth Gap—and How to Address It* (Washington, DC: Brookings Institution, June 2019), https://www.brookings.edu/blog/brookings-now/2019/06/18/a-conversation-about-the-racial-wealth-gap-and-how-to-address-it.

2. Zack Friedman, "Student Loan Debt Statistics in 2020: A Record $1.6 Trillion," *Forbes*, February 3, 2020, https://www.forbes.com/sites/zackfriedman/2020/02/03/student-loan-debt-statistics/#4545c51c281f.

3. Lindsey Reichlin Cruse, MA, Tessa Holtzman, Barbara Gault, PhD, David Croom, and Portia Polk, *Student Parents by the Numbers*, Institute for Women's Policy Research, April 11, 2019, https://iwpr.org/iwpr-issues/student-parent-success-initiative/parents-in-college-by-the-numbers.

4. "Single Student Parents Have Higher Student Debt Burden, Especially at For-Profit Colleges," Institute for Women's Policy Research, May 30, 2012, https://iwpr.org/media/press-releases/single-student-parents-have-higher-student-debt-burden-especially-at-for-profit-colleges.

5. Christina Cauterucci, "More Single Mothers Are Going to College Than Ever. But Very Few Will Graduate," *Slate*, September 22, 2017, https://slate.com/human-interest/2017/09/for-profit-schools-and-low-graduation-rates-plague-a-rising-population-of-single-student-mothers.html.

6. Victoria Jackson and Tiffany Jones, "The 'Black Tax' Is Key to Understanding and Solving the Black Student Debt Crisis in the Time of COVID-19 and Beyond,"

The Education Trust, April 16, 2020, https://edtrust.org/resource/the-black-tax
-is-key-to-understanding-and-solving-the-black-student-debt-crisis-in-the-time-of
-covid-19-and-beyond.

CHAPTER 15: BREECH

1. Kathryn Kost and Stanley Henshaw, *U.S. Teenage Pregnancies, Births and Abortions, 2008: State Trends by Age, Race and Ethnicity* (New York: Guttmacher Institute, March 2013), https://www.guttmacher.org/sites/default/files/pdfs/pubs/USTPtrends State08.pdf.

2. Jennifer Manlove, Elizabeth Cook, Mae Cooper, August Aldebot-Green, and Kate Welti, "Location Matters: Geographic Variation in Teen Childbearing Within Washington, D.C.," Child Trends, November 1, 2014, https://www.childtrends.org /publications/location-matters.

3. "Child Poverty by Ward in District of Columbia," Annie E. Casey Foundation, Kids Count Data Center, 2018, https://datacenter.kidscount.org/data/tables/6748 -child-poverty-by-ward#detailed/21/1852–1859/false/37,871,870,573,869,36,868 ,867,133,11/any/13834.

4. "Ward 8, DC," Census Reporter, 2018, https://censusreporter.org/profiles /61000US11008-ward-8-dc.

CHAPTER 16: CEO

1. "State Unemployment Rates in 2010," US Bureau of Labor and Statistics, March 1, 2011, https://www.bls.gov/opub/ted/2011/ted_20110301.htm#:~:text=The %20U.S.%20jobless%20rate%20was,of%2010.0%20percent%20or%20more.

2. Cyndi Suarez, "The Nonprofit Racial Leadership Gap: Flipping the Lens," *Nonprofit Quarterly*, June 8, 2017, https://nonprofitquarterly.org/nonprofit-racial-leadership -gap-flipping-lens/#:~:text=For%20over%20a%20decade%20now,executive%20 leadership%20emerged%20early%20on.

3. *Giving in the Greater Washington Region*, Washington Regional Association of Grantmakers, November 12, 2019, https://www.washingtongrantmakers.org/sites /default/files/resources/2019%20Our%20Region%2C%20Our%20Giving.pdf.

4. Brian Schwartz, "Robin Hood Foundation Launches New Initiative Aimed at Funding Nonprofits Run Only by People of Color," CNBC, June 30, 2020, https:// www.cnbc.com/2020/07/01/robin-hood-foundation-launches-fund-to-help-groups -run-by-people-of-color.html.

5. Vanessa Daniel, "Philanthropists Bench Women of Color, the M.V.P.s of Social Change," *New York Times*, November 19, 2019, https://www.nytimes.com/2019/11/19 /opinion/philanthropy-black-women.html.

6. Alexandria Walton Radford, Melissa Cominole, and Paul Skomsvold, "Demographic and Enrollment Characteristics of Nontraditional Undergraduates: 2011–12," US RTI International, September 2015, http://nces.ed.gov/pubsearch/pubsinfo.asp ?pubid=2015025.

7. Elissa Nadworny, "College Completion Rates Are Up, but the Numbers Will Still Surprise You," NPR, March 13, 2019, https://www.npr.org/2019/03/13/681621047 /college-completion-rates-are-up-but-the-numbers-will-still-surprise-you.

8. Elizabeth Noll, PhD, Lindsey Reichlin, MA, and Barbara Gault, PhD, "College Students with Children: National and Regional Profiles," Institute for Women's Policy Research, January 2017, https://iwpr.org/iwpr-issues/student-parent-success-initiative/college-students-with-children-national-and-regional-profiles.

9. Pearl Stewart, "Campus Child Care Critical in Raising Single Mothers' Graduation Rates," *Diverse Issues in Higher Education*, June 6, 2018, https://diverseeducation.com/article/117704.

10. Julia B. Isaacs, *Starting School at a Disadvantage: The School Readiness of Poor Children* (Washington, DC: Brookings Institution, March 2012), https://www.brookings.edu/wp-content/uploads/2016/06/0319_school_disadvantage_isaacs.pdf.